How to use marketing to survive and thrive in economically turbulent times

Catrina Clulow FCIM Chartered Marketer

Thrive, Not Just Survive

© Copyright Catrina Clulow 2024 – All Rights Reserved

The content contained within this book may not be reproduced, duplicated or transmitted without direct written permission from the author.

Under no circumstances will any blame or legal responsibility be held against the author or publisher for any damages, reparation, or monetary loss due to the information contained within this book. Either directly or indirectly.

Legal Notice

This book is copyrighted protected. You cannot amend, distribute, sell, use, quote or paraphrase any part of the content within this book without the consent of the author.

Disclaimer Notice

All effort has been made to present accurate, up to date, and reliable, complete information. No warranties of any kind are declared or implied. Readers acknowledge that the author is not engaging in the rendering of legal, financial, medical or professional advice. The content within this book has been derived from various sources.

By reading this document, the reader agrees that under no circumstances is the author responsible for any losses, direct or indirect, which are incurred as a result of the use of the information contained within this document, including, but not limited to – errors, omissions and inaccuracies.

Contents

About the Author 11
Who is this book for? 13
Introduction 15
   Understanding the current economic turmoil. 15
      What is the difference between a recession and a period of negative growth? 17
   What can I do as a business owner or leader? 21
      Are there any quick fixes? 25
      Won't price drops help? 25
      Looking at your other customers 27
Section I: Laying the Foundation 31
   Let's take a detailed look at your own business. 33
      How are your numbers looking? 33
      Know your offerings 33
      Set meaningful and achievable targets. 35
      Clear Mission & Vision Statements 35
      Flexibility 40
   Embracing a Marketing Mindset 43
      What is Marketing anyway? 43
      What is a marketing mindset? 44
      A brief overview of the marketing Ps. 44
      What do all the Ps mean in brief? 45
      I don't want all those Ps. How else can I define Marketing? 52
      Summary 56
   Defining your target audience 57

DMU elements / persona development 61

Crafting Your Unique Selling Proposition (USP) 67

Setting SMART Marketing Goals: Creating measurable and achievable marketing objectives. 71

Section II: Marketing in Turbulent Times 75

Communication Flows 77

Social Media, Organic 79

    LinkedIn 82

    Twitter / X / Threads / Mastodon 87

    Facebook / Instagram 87

    Others: TikTok, Snapchat, Pinterest 88

Social Media Paid For 91

SEM 95

SEO 99

Website 103

Email marketing 109

    Lead nurturing 110

    Relationship marketing including newsletters 112

    Specific campaigns 113

    Tools needed 113

Direct mail 115

Advertising 119

    Display Online 119

    Offline 120

    OOH (Outdoor) 120

    Radio 123

PR 125
   Press Releases 125
   Articles / Opinion Pieces 127
   Blogs 127
   Case Studies (written and video) 128
   Testimonials (written and video) 131
   White Papers 131
   Podcasts 132
   E books 132
Events 133
   Exhibitions 134
   Seminars and Workshops 135
   Conferences 139
   Webinars 140
Market Intelligence / Surveys 143
Relationship Marketing 145
Word of Mouth Marketing and Referrals 149
Loyalty Schemes 151
Sales Promotions 153
Internal Marketing 157
Integrating the tools together for better results 161
Partnering for Success 163
   What is a strategic alliance and why are they important? 163
   Resellers & Distributors 164
Section III: Marketing Measurement and Adaptation 167

Key Marketing Metrics to Monitor: Identifying and tracking essential performance indicators .. 169

Agile Marketing in a Turbulent Environment: How to adapt your marketing strategies to changing economic conditions. 179

    Customer Feedback: 183

    Market Research 191

        Competitor analysis 192

        PESTLE 193

        Product Need & Market Sizing 195

Conclusion 197

Index 199

Figures

Figure 1: BCG Matrix Example _____ *34*
Figure 2: 2 and 3 tier IT channels _____ *48*
Figure 3: An Example Why Cascade _____ *55*
Figure 4: Simplified Buyer Persona Matrix _____ *59*
Figure 5: Vertical Markets and Horizontal Markets _____ *60*
Figure 6: SMART Goal Definitions _____ *71*
Figure 7: Sample Communication Flow for an IT Vendor *77*
Figure 8: Communication Flows in UK Healthcare _____ *78*
Figure 9: Web Address Dos and Don'ts _____ *106*
Figure 10: Maltese Cross with Panels Numbered as Seen When Opened _____ *116*
Figure 11: The SCRAP Format _____ *130*
Figure 12: Bow-tie structure, with one example of functions, the left is the customer, the right is your company. _____ *147*
Figure 13: Diamond Structure, with same sample functions as above. _____ *147*
Figure 14: Combining the marketing mix together _____ *161*
Figure 15: Conversion rate implications _____ *176*
Figure 16: The constant improvement cycle _____ *177*
Figure 17: Net Promoter Score Categories _____ *186*
Figure 18: Net Promoter Score Calculation _____ *187*

Tables

Table 1: Feature Benefit Table Example.......................... 68
Table 2: Sample LinkedIn Hashtag Volumes................. 86
Table 3: What to measure and what not to measure .. 171
Table 4: First Example of a NPS Score 187
Table 5: Second Example of a NPS Score 188

About the Author

Catrina Clulow is a Chartered Marketer and a Fellow of the Chartered Institute of Marketing with over 30 years of experience in international B2B marketing, predominantly in the IT sector.

Before she set up her own consultancy business, she had a successful career in companies ranging from start-ups through to multi-national enterprises. The latter she refers to as "corporate land".

Her consultancy helps mainly start-up, microbusinesses and small companies. That is her first love. As it is where she knows whatever she suggests is going to make a big impact on her client's bottom line.

She has lived and breathed marketing taking businesses through recessions and turbulent times in the past.

If this book throws up questions that you need help with, book a 30-minute free of charge call with Catrina: https://calendly.com/cutthrough/introductory-call nothing to lose, everything to gain or drop her a line on ctc@cutthrough.marketing

Who is this book for?

This book aims to help those who have not worked through a global recession before (it is 14 years since the financial crash after all and the world is a whole lot different from then) or such a period of economic turbulence that we have seen during and since the pandemic.

It is also for those who have limited knowledge about marketing.

It is written trying to avoid jargon with tips and tricks that will help your business survive, thrive and be as successful as it can be.

Introduction

Understanding the current economic turmoil.

"As sure as the spring will follow the winter, prosperity and economic growth will follow recession."

- Bo Bennett

These last couple of years have been a real rollercoaster, haven't they?

The pandemic caused a lot of issues. People couldn't go into work in many cases. Hospitality was shut down. New ways of working had to be found. Shipping pretty much ceased so supply chains were heavily disrupted.

The pandemic also saw the drop in prices of various raw materials. At one point the author even filled the car up at 99p per litre! Now come on that was just unreal.

Since the pandemic, the roller coaster hasn't got any less bumpy and scary.

First of all we had the high.

Yes, we were let out of our homes, we could meet up again. We treated ourselves to a few new clothes after living in the same elasticated waisted things the comfort eating led to some people having to size up in their wardrobes.

It looked like the economy was going to do a lovely V shape.

But the supply chain was still all over the place. Docks were full of empty containers in the European ports, and there was a shortage of containers in the Far East.

Some countries kept their lockdowns for longer.

Everything that had been put on hold suddenly came off hold. All at the same time. That led to inflationary pressures on raw materials. Everywhere. Globally.

For many, days of double-digit inflation were unknown. For those of us a bit older then memories of parents struggling dominated childhood. My Mum worked three part-time jobs and my Dad had a full-time and a part-time job. He also grew pretty much all our vegetables and fruit for the year (a lovely big chest freezer helped that).

To control the inflation, central banks have increased interest rates. Ouch! That has been painful both for individuals and businesses. Of course, in reality, those interest rates have merely returned to a more normal level BUT we have just had over a decade of near zero rates due to the financial crisis.

Many commenters spoke about recessions coming down the line. That in itself can cause recessions as people and businesses hold on to cash for a rainy day.

Then the same commenters say that a recession is unlikely in the UK but that it will be a year of negative growth. Huh? Then those same commenters say that there won't be a reduction in the economy in 2023 after all but could be in 2024 – things start getting taken off hold by some, but with all this flip-flopping back and forth true confidence has not come back yet.

One major reason for that is the Ukraine situation. It wasn't just the end of the pandemic that caused oil to increase in price, but the war in

Ukraine. Followed by the sanctions on Russia. The problem in getting the wheat and sunflower oil out of Ukraine.

What happens if Russia accidentally has a missile hit a NATO country? What happens if as well as Ukraine Putin turns his mind to other countries that he believes are rightfully part of Russia?

More recently we have had the Israelis going into the Gaza Strip after they were attacked. There is a fear that the Middle East more broadly could erupt, and there are little signs of that as ships are targeted in the Gulf if there is a suspicion that they are going to Israel, or sometimes the UK and the US.

That means that the Cape route is being taken which adds time and costs on to the supply chain.

Something that has affected the UK specifically, is the political uncertainty which followed Boris Johnson's resignation. Instead of focusing on moving the country forwards, Government had a spat amongst itself.

Never a good thing.

Then we had the chaos caused by the Mini Budget. Another leadership contest. Credibility of the country hit, and hit hard. The pound sunk. Imports became even more expensive. Inflation was increased. Forecasts were that the recession could last 2 years at one point.

All of this has led to a period of economic uncertainty not seen for a very long time.

What is the difference between a recession and a period of negative growth?

Of course, there is the dictionary definition of what a recession is, but that can also alter by country. Here in the UK it is formally *"a recession when the economy has contracted for two successive quarters."*

What does that actually mean?

There isn't just one economy there are different sectors that perform at different levels. Often the headlines will break it down a little: services were down, construction was up, manufacturing was down, retail was down and so on.

Again, those are such wide brush strokes of sectors. In services there is everything from your local hairdresser through to the very large accountancy and legal companies. The same applies to retail. There are some many different segments to retail from your local independent bakery to a high-end art gallery. The chances are that each are seeing different effects.

But there is another issue with the definition: it is two successive quarters of negative growth or contraction.

That means that the country only "officially" knows that is in recession when it has already been in a recession for two quarters – six months is a long time to be unsure of something in business.

As we discussed above, it can also lead to a self-fulfilling prophecy. People think in month one of quarter one that things don't feel as buoyant as they would like. This feeling continues in months two and three, but business continues as originally planned.

Then the media use the R word as a possibility.

That is a great way to really effect the economy.

That feeling is suddenly named. Behaviour changes in many cases.

Those behaviour changes, putting off buying that new server or renewing the retainer with the legal company, all have a knock-on effect.

By protecting your own company's cashflow, then the cashflow of the supplier is reduced, so they cancel various expenditure items of their own and so the vicious circle continues until all sections of the economy are affected.

No-one is saying that money can be spent if it isn't there, but before cancelling that planned expenditure, ask why it should be cancelled. Is the positive impact that you were projecting not going to be there for productivity, efficiency, sales gains?

It could very well be that the money is having to go on to increased utility bills, higher wages and salaries, more expensive raw materials.

It could be that you are trying to absorb as many of these costs as possible to avoid price rises to your customers, which in turn would fuel inflation.

After all recession in the 2020s is a different beast to the financial crash, or the recessions in the 1970s, 1980s and 1990s, for all the reasons discussed above.

Without the war in Ukraine fuelling the inflationary pressure, then that could have been quite short-term. But for the first time in 70 years war was added into the mix in Europe.

On 24 February 2022, Russia invaded Ukraine.

To try and avoid an escalation into World War Three, the EU, the UK, the US and others laid sanctions on Russia.

Russia has replied by reducing the amount of gas that it is sending through the Nord Stream I pipeline – affecting businesses and individuals.

The EU attempts to find supplies from elsewhere. The price of gas shoots through the roof. Electricity in the UK goes through the roof taking money out of the consumer's disposable income and paring back profit margins at businesses.

As inflation soared to over 10% the Bank of England raised interest rates, making borrowings that firms and individuals had more and more expensive.

Just as importantly it makes the Government's debt, which increased enormously during the pandemic, have a far higher interest rate. That debt becomes more expensive and therefore tax cuts which were forecast are also cancelled.

This is not just affecting one country. The inflation is global. The interest rate increases are being encouraged by the IMF, and have been since December 2021.

Negative growth is where an economy is smaller at the end of the year than at the beginning, but because there haven't been two successive quarters, then the official R word cannot be used. Still not good news though, is it?

That dear reader is where we are leaving the doom and gloom behind. Think positively and positive things happen!

Thrive, Not Just Survive

What can I do as a business owner or leader?

Money grows on the tree of persistence
– Japanese Proverb

First things first: Don't panic!

Don't get caught up in the negativity that the media enjoys concentrating on. Good news is never as interesting for them as the bad news stories are.

There is the old adage that the only constant in life is change. A recession is a type of change, and whatever you do, don't wait for "normal" business to resume. Yesterday's normal is vastly different from tomorrow's normal.

During turbulent times there are two ways of riding out the storm. Both have their risks. Either may be right for you and your business.

Batten Down the Hatches

You may decide to stay in a safe harbour to avoid the tall waves and deep troughs that can sink a ship at times. You batten down the hatches. Concentrate on your core offerings. Concentrate on just surviving through and not becoming a victim of the economic turbulence. You use conservative cashflow management, as cash is king in your head.

There is absolutely nothing wrong with doing that.

But for many companies it means coming out of the downturn takes longer. When they do put the head above the parapet then they do not recognise the new environment, the new market. That could slow them down or could even be their death knell. Even if you decide to follow this strategy, then do keep an eye on how the market is changing so that you can react in a timely manner and don't get caught out.

Use the winds to your advantage.

What is one company's harsh winds can be another company's assisting winds. It all depends on the viewpoint and the flexibility that the company has in tacking the sails to harness the wind.

For example, during the pandemic, various boutique spirit manufacturers saw their sales of their spirits drop. People don't drink as much at home compared to a night out with friends.

The distilleries could have shut up shop and put their staff on furlough. But a significant number decided to use their alcohol making skills in a different way. They decided to produce hand sanitizers. A product which saw an enormous growth where supply was being outstripped by demand.

Not only did the distilleries keep their staff employed, but they also played their part in beating the virus.

The luxury clothing brand Burberry moved their production lines to making PPE clothing for the NHS. The first 100,000 items Burberry donated and was then given a contract worth £573,000.[1]

Not only did these companies survive the lockdowns, but they also helped their supply chains survive. Most importantly, from a branding point of view, they showed that they were ready to support the common and greater cause of protecting the population from Covid-19.

---

[1] https://www.bbc.co.uk/news/uk-england-leeds-54001950

During the financial crash, we saw the birth of popular peer-to-peer lending, as the banks could not support small businesses, and as we all know, cashflow is king for survival.

The original market entrant in the UK was Zopa in 2005, followed by Lending Club and Prosper in the US in 2006.[2] So before the financial crash, but they came into their own by grasping the opportunity when presented.

These platforms used technology to help people lend from other people side-lining the financial institutions. As trust in those institutions was deeply affected by the financial crash of 2008, such platforms saw massive growth. By 2021 Zopa exited the peer-to-peer lending market, it became a bank itself.[3]

Funding Circle, the key P2P platform in the UK now, was founded in August 2010[4] in response to the distrust that there was for the banks. Since 2013, Funding Circle has received funds from the UK Government to lend to small businesses.[5] During the pandemic, Funding Circle became a main supplier of Coronavirus Business Interruption Loan Scheme (CBILS) and the Recovery Loan Scheme.

---

[2] https://www.iuvo-group.com/en/history-peer-to-peer-lending-platforms-3/

[3] https://www.theguardian.com/money/2021/dec/11/zopa-peer-to-peer-lending-p2p-money

[4] https://www.fundingcircle.com/uk/about-us/

[5] https://www.fundingcircle.com/uk/small-business-loans/government-business-loans/

By taking the negative winds and leveraging them, small or start-up companies can become major organisations.

Uber was founded in March 2009.[6] Mobility as a platform is how they describe their offering, but they also could take advantage of individuals who needed work and also had access to a car. The Uber trips were also cheaper than a regular taxi or mini cab so in those recessionary times a habit started. A habit which has now spread to over 70 countries. They also used speed to enable growth before countries could respond with how Uber could be controlled. Taxis are regulated. Uber put itself forward as a technology company.

Airbnb is another company founded in the Financial Crisis.[7] People still wanted to travel but hotels were too expensive. People had spare rooms, annexes or apartments that were unused assets. Airbnb allows those that want to travel to save money while the host earns money.

What do all these examples show us? That even in recessionary or turbulent times there are opportunities.

When an economy contracts by 5% there is still 95% of it available. That is something that you need to keep in your mind at all times. So far, the UK economy is not predicted to formally go into recession, but it is expected that the economy will either end 2023 0.1% lower than the start or be flat. Not all sectors will contract at the same rate, and even within those sectors there is always a great spread of results.

---

[6] https://en.wikipedia.org/wiki/Uber

[7] https://en.wikipedia.org/wiki/Airbnb

In short, concentrate on the opportunities, but keep an eye on any threats. That way you can grow your business and protect it at the same time.

Are there any quick fixes?

If you are thinking that increasing social media will solve all your challenges, then sorry to tell you, that there is no one marketing panacea to solve all ills.

That is not to say that social media and digital marketing will not have a role to play in your marketing mix, but how much of a role will vary from company to company.

Won't price drops help?

Well in these days of inflation, maintaining prices could be a major feat on its own.

BUT

Before you rely on pricing as a way to come through. Carefully consider if you are in danger of alienating your target market.

For example, if you are a business consultant who normally charges £1000 a day, if you suddenly dropped your fees to £500 a day, would your target audience treat you the same? Probably not. The fee reduction would put doubt into their minds as to whether you were the right person for them.

Price reductions can also lose you profitable business.

If you enter into a price war with other companies, then that can quickly lead to commoditisation of your offerings. In a price war no-one wins: it reduces profits. It can lead to market consolidation, and in the end, it is the end customer who loses out.

You need to be clear what the value of your offering is and why the price or fee charged is more than fair.

In downturns, it is the middle-positioned products and services that lose out. Their clients can downgrade to a cheaper option if their purse strings are tightening.

Alternatively, some will upgrade to the upper end products and services, as they "treat" themselves to cope with the pressures of the inflation, increased interest rates and general stresses that come along with economic turbulence.

If you are in that middle stratum, you need to work harder to keep your clients loyal to you. Maybe you actually launch a new upper-level service that your current clients can aspire to.

Does that sound counterintuitive to you? Going for more expensive solutions instead of going to the bottom of the market?

It may be a lot easier than you think. It is always worth considering. That upper-level offering can still be there once the economic turbulence has finished with us. It can lead to good growth once the economy normalises.

Take a look at what the supermarkets are doing at the moment. Sainsbury's and Tesco are both price matching Aldi for hundreds of products.

Why?

To ensure that their clients do not move their whole weekly shop to Aldi whilst the cost-of-living crisis is reigning. The big supermarkets would need to fight to get it back again afterwards.

Better to grab the headlines with the price matching so that loyal shoppers stay loyal. There is always the chance that they will stay with the middle range of some products or even upgrade to the Taste the Difference or Finest ranges for others.

When you look at it, Sainsbury's and Tesco offer thousands of products. Not just the hundreds that they are price matching.

It may appear that in the short term, they are gambling a slight reduction in profits will be offset with the additional top-level items that they sell, the additional visit to their café or the additional grocery items not covered by the price match.

BUT

In reality, they are taking a long-term view of the market. They are fighting to remain in the top 4 largest supermarkets. They are all too well aware of the shopper's that they lost during the 2008/09 financial crisis and recession who have never returned.

You need to look at the impacts of any price promotions that you do and ensure that they are for the benefit of your company in the long-term not just the next few months.

If pricing isn't where the answer is, then how can you ensure that you will not only survive but also grow during the recession?

Looking at your other customers

In reality that shouldn't say customers but those customers who are not purchasers instead they are stakeholders, but who likes jargon?

Well, there are a couple of categories that can make or break what happens in the near future just as easily as your purchasers.

Your suppliers

Surely, you are a customer of theirs? Well yes you are. At the same time, they are fundamental to your success.

They care whether you can survive and grow – as it has a fundamental impact on their own business.

Now if you are a small company, don't undervalue what your business means even to the large utility companies or business banks out there.

If you have an account manager, reach out and make sure that they know exactly what it is that you do.

Why?

Because they can give your name to another client struggling with the exact problem you can solve. They need their customers to be successful so that they stay successful.

If you don't ask, if you don't push yourself forwards, someone else will do so and take those referrals.

It makes business sense as well. Remember people do business with people. If, heaven forbid, you did have an issue with your own company's cashflow then having a good relationship with a person can help smooth troubled waters more easily.

For your smaller suppliers, they can be just as valuable for referrals. Maybe you could even do some joint marketing activities so that you both spend less but have more impact.

To keep those suppliers afloat, which is in your own interests to do so, then ensure that all your payments are on time, or even early. Help them remove some of the stress by being an ethical customer, an ethical company.

Word will get around and suppliers will want to work with you in the future. It could lead to better discounts. It could lead to better payment terms.

Retailers or channel partners

If you sell through retailers or channel partners and you see that they are struggling with cashflow, and if you can afford it, then how about you give them a stocking order that they only have to pay for in 12 months' time?

Have you got a confused look on your face now?

Well consider this, if they have products then they can sell them. The replacement stock will be ordered and paid for as normal from the cash that they took.

If they have the choice of two companies to stock, then you are going to be a preferred partner going forwards as you helped them, and they will give your products the focus and best shelf positions.

Local Government

You may be wondering how your local borough or county council can help you.

Well, they have a vested interest in helping you be successful.

One way that they can do this, if you're a business who wants to invest in apprentices but your business is below the levy level, is to match you up with companies who will not be spending their levy.

The council can help to introduce you to your local branch of The Apprenticeship & Skills Partnership who help move the apprenticeship levy through an initiative called Transfer to Transform.[8]

---

[8] https://www.theapprenticeshiphub.com/transfer-to-transform/

Investing in your staff by training can give job security plus it increases morale. Not all apprenticeships are at the starter level, some are degree level. By using such schemes the cost to your organisation is mitigated but you have the benefit of the new skills for moving your company forwards.

Sometimes such schemes are run by Chambers of Commerce too.

Reach out and never be afraid to ask for help which is out there ready and waiting for you to come along.

So let's look at everything in a lot more detail.

Section I: Laying the Foundation

"We need to accept that we won't always make the right decisions, that we'll screw up royally sometimes — understanding that failure is not the opposite of success, it's part of success.

- Arianna Huffington, Founder & CEO, Thrive Global

Thrive, Not Just Survive

Let's take a detailed look at your own business.

"If you don't know your numbers, you don't know your business."

- Marcus Lemonis

How are your numbers looking?

If you need to make changes to forecasts and budgets, then do it once if at all possible. (Ok the author is just breaking out in a cold sweat remembering the amount of work that having multiple marketing budget cuts was during the financial crisis. Doing it once would have allowed time being spent on positive items instead of the negative. Each cut came later in the year so monies had been spent which may have been spent differently if the truth had been known up front – of course you don't have a crystal ball but be decisive – it is a lot easier to release additional funds than cut.)

Know your profitability, your margins.

Know your cashflow projections.

Know the impact of a 10% increase on wages and salaries.

Know where the red flag action points are ahead of time so that when they arrive you know the actions that need taking.

Know your offerings

Know which ones are the most profitable. Which ones are relevant to your targets. Which ones offer you growth, which ones are at the end of the product life cycle.

One of the most frequently used ways of describing products or services is the Boston Consulting Group (BCG), with their dogs, question marks, problem child, rising stars and cash cows.

Most people have heard of a cash cow. In this sense it is a product or service that doesn't need much investment to bring in profitable sales. A business' holy grail. But what are the others?

BCG drew up this matrix years ago to help identify where to spend the marketing money, the R&D money, the sales effort, which products and services to keep and which to quietly let die.

In the diagram below you will see a two-by-two square, the bottom axis is low market share to high market share; the vertical access is low market growth to high market growth. It seems very simple, but it can be a very powerful analysis tool.

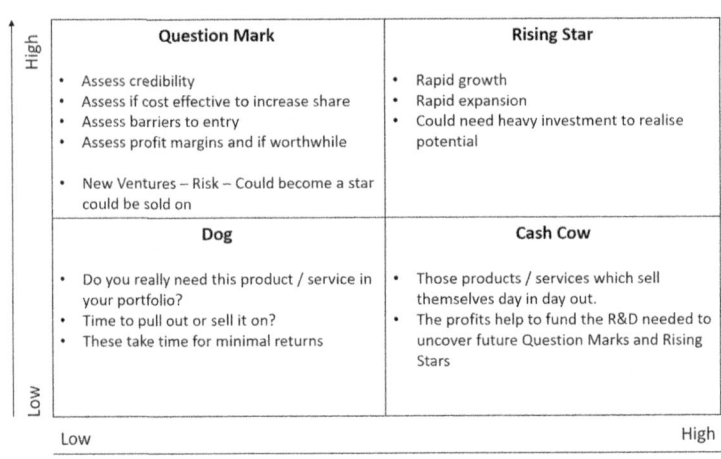

Figure 1: BCG Matrix Example

Question marks and problem child (the kid can make good, or the kid can go down a bad path) refer to the same quadrant.

Thrive, Not Just Survive

Take a little time and be harsh / fair about which of your products and services sit where today and where you think they are going in the future. Which question marks could become a rising star, which are heading to dogs; which rising stars today are going to be your cash cows of the future?

Yes, it is a bit of jargon using those specific terms, but the positioning of yourself against your competitors can make a difference to focus, one that you hadn't noticed until you spend a few minutes mapping it all out. It will help you prioritise, something which will benefit your business growth going forwards, possibly a better work life balance too. It helps you be more objective.

Set meaningful and achievable targets.

Involve everyone in the business and remind how everyone can help during difficult times.

Remind everyone that the small things can all add up to a big impact. Whether it is something as simple as reminding the last person out to turn off the lights. Putting bonuses in place based on company profits. Focus on the sales that are still there with internal marketing campaigns (more on that later).

Overall, remind yourself, your managers and every worker in the business, that even if the overall economy contracts 5%, that is huge, but there is still the 95% out there.

To be success in a period of economic turmoil, you have to outperform your competitors. Don't follow their strategies, follow your own based on your own goals.

Clear Mission & Vision Statements

Your mission statement should be where your business is today. It sums up your company, why you are in business, what your aims are, what your product or service is, who your primary customers are and geography you work in.

Sounds not so bad, but it has to be done in one to three sentences and in around 30-60 words maximum.

Share it with your staff – it does help focus the mind. So ensure that everybody understands your mission statement. It is the core of the business, the elevator pitch in many ways. If they understand this then they should know exactly what your business is about and know if what they are doing fits with the company's aims or not.

Especially important in turbulent times.

Let's take a look at a couple of mission statements and see how they hold together:

Apple: "*We believe that we are on the face of the earth to make great products and that's not changing. We are here to make the best products on earth, and to leave the world better than we found it.*"

With this mission statement Apple are clear that they are global. That they believe that they have superior products, and that is always the aim, so customers can feel confident in their investment in Apple's products.

They give their rationale for existence as being to produce the best anywhere in the world. Then they hint at their CSR (Corporate Social Responsibility) aspects – they want to leave the world better than they found it – that has environmental overtones, but also the way that they care for their staff making their lives better, and also that their products make the world better for their users.

That last one depends on screen addiction, but think about the dementia sufferer that has alarms and to do lists on their iPhone or iPad to maintain their independence or the woman desperate to be a Mum who uses a cycle tracking app to see when she is at her most fertile.

Apple have covered a lot in two sentences and 39 words.

Netflix's mission statement is a little longer: *"At Netflix, we want to entertain the world. Whatever your taste, and no matter where you live, we give you access to best-in-class TV shows, movies and documentaries. Our members control what they want to watch, when they want it, with no ads, in one simple subscription."*

This time the two sentences have 47 words. It is evident that this mission statement is aimed squarely at clients and prospects by using the second person combined with the first person. They use the word members to imply a kind of club, a community, not a customer, but someone who controls what they watch and by their feedback help Netflix to define what to produce more of. Again, a company with global aims, and they active in 190 countries, so they are delivering on that aim. However, since 2023 the "with no ads" bit is not always the case depending on the membership type chosen

Now let's look at a very short mission statement from Gucci: *"The company's mission is to become the leader in luxury market at worldwide level."*

Just one sentence with 14 words. It is short, to the point, but does it really cover all the aspects that a mission statement should cover? Looking at the 10 words after *"the company's mission is"* they have a clear aim in a clear geography, but they don't really state who their client base is, yes, they say luxury, but that is not a client base is it? It may be that someone saves up for a one-off piece, or they could be high net worth individuals who buy as a matter of course.

Of course, luxury is also subjective depending where in the world and which demographic you are looking at.

The mission statement assumes that the reader knows quite a lot about Gucci to start off with, as they don't define which element of the luxury market, they want to be the leader in, after all they don't manufacture cars, private jets, yachts or handmade bespoke kitchens as some examples. This mission statement doesn't really hit what it should do.

What to consider when developing your own mission statement:

1. **Action**: Use active voice for urgency, not passive voice.
2. **Simplicity**: Avoid all jargon and buzzwords – it has to be understood by all readers not just those in your business or your sector.
3. **Growth**: Allow room to grow in the future. Don't have a mission statement that restricts you or your staff.
4. **Personality**: Your mission statement needs to show the personality of your business.
5. **Forward-looking**: Remember to look at the bigger picture: none of the examples above state current facts about the business but what they are aiming for.

Your vision statement is where you want your business to be in the future, it is where you are going in the next 5-10 years. It will be idealistic – because who knows what the future holds for us, if we did then life would be so much more boring and maybe even scary.

This does give some more leeway, but it still needs to be short and succinct. A similar 30 – 60 words in length, written in the present tense even though it is for the future. Ambitious, but not off the scale. Link back to your USPs and your mission statement.

US firm Warby Parker have the following vision statement: "*We believe that buying glasses should be easy and fun. It should leave you happy and good-looking, with money in your pocket. We also believe that everyone has the right to see.*"

Within 32 words, it is clear that they are selling cost-effective spectacles so that everyone can have clear eyesight. The emphasis on fun and good-looking also points to their younger demographic.

Rhythm, a surfing equipment brand, has the following vision statement: *"To pave our own way as a leading alternative surf, swim and lifestyle brand in a market dominated by large commercial surf brands. To design premium products that are made for a coastal lifestyle and bring the brand story to life through products captured in an authentic, creative and realistic light."*

They appreciate that they are a smaller player in the market, but that they want to be more unique. At 51 words it is a little longer than Warby Parker's but is still clear where they are aiming to be.

Some vision statements are much shorter. The following is from Oxfam: *"A world without poverty."*

Those four words sum up exactly what Oxfam is attempting to do. They are ambitious, but one would hope that they are also achievable.

Unilever's vision statement points towards their ESG (environmental social governance) responsibilities: *"To grow our business, while decoupling our environmental footprint from our growth and increasing our positive social impact."*

Eighteen words that mean that staff and customers can hold them accountable for their environmental footprint.

Flexibility

If the pandemic has taught us as business owners and leaders anything, it is that we need to be flexible.

We need to be able to pivot and adapt.

Use those pandemic skills now that we are in this turmoil.

If you have staff who can work from home, and want to work from home, then allow them to do so. It fosters loyalty from them, but also allows them to save on commuting costs, so reduces the pressure on salaries.

In addition, you save the costs of having a person on site – just count up the real costs of someone being in the office, from the power the laptop uses to the drinks machine being used more to heating and lighting offices, which could be empty and the rent saved, to the basic essentials such as loo paper and soap.

These days you do not want presentism, it is severely frowned upon, instead you want to have motivated staff to ensure the company continues to move forwards. Trust and empower your staff and they will deliver for you.

Having said that, encourage ideas from everyone in the organisation.

It doesn't matter who has the idea, there is the folklore story most of us have heard. A cosmetics company wanted to increase sales of its shampoo products. They asked outside experts and consultants. They asked all their workers. It was a man on the shopfloor who said, "why not add the word Repeat to the bottle."

It may just be a story, but it shows how the simplest suggestions can add sales. Another story, this time a true one, is about how suggestions can help to reduce costs.

Back in the early 1900s Swan Vesta wanted to increase profits. Again, a junior person said that they had an idea to decrease production costs. He wasn't taken seriously at first, but eventually he was given time to present his idea. He suggested putting the sandpaper on one side of the matchbox instead of two. That decreased the expenditure on glue and sandpaper.

Today we are seeing pressure from outside of companies to make a difference to how they run and to the products including packaging.

Think about the main food retailers.

They are all now reducing packaging and plastic overall.

Yes, environmental change is causing some of this. But also, they have worked out how much money they can save.

If things are more efficiently packaged, then more can be fitted in a box, more goods on one truck.

If less plastic is needed, less plastic is purchased. If the bag of ready washed salad is slightly smaller but the contents are the same, then the gas injected is also reduced.

If less packaging is needed for the truck transportation, then they have less packaging to dispose of, which in turn reduces their costs.

Moving to 4x concentrated squash, as Sainsbury's have done, means the same shelf space earns double the turnover (well actually slightly more as they managed to put a price increase in there at launch even though their costs have decreased). In retail real estate is king, so having more turnover from the same space is fantastic.

Listen to your staff.

Listen to your customers.

They may just have the ideas that you need during these turbulent times and then when the better times come back your profits will continue to rise.

Embracing a Marketing Mindset

> *"The world as we have created it is a process of our thinking. It cannot be changed without changing our thinking"*
>
> *- Albert Einstein*

Marketing is not just colouring pens and pretty pictures. It is something that can get to the real essence of a company when done correctly. Let's explore more:

What is Marketing anyway?

It is quite simple to define the wrong answer: Advertising. Marketing is so much more than advertising.

There is the American Marketing Association answer: *Marketing is the process of planning and executing the conception, pricing, promotion and distribution of ideas, goods and services to create exchange and satisfy individual and organizational objectives.*

There is the definition from Theodore Levitt: *Selling focuses on the needs of the seller; marketing on the needs of the buyer. Selling is preoccupied with the seller's need to convert his product into cash; marketing with the idea of satisfying the needs of the customer by means of the product and the whole cluster of things associated with creating, delivering and finally consuming it.*

Then there is this answer: *Marketing is about informing the right people about my product or service at the right time in the right way and at the right fee.*

What is a marketing mindset?

For a company to have a marketing mindset, it is all about putting the customer front and centre. In the past we have seen engineering led companies – here's a product now who wants it. Marketing led companies ask the customers what it is that they need to make their lives better or easier and then they go and produce that product or service at the price point that the customers have already said that they would be happy with.

By having a marketing mindset, then money is not wasted on products that will never take off. Sinclair C5 is a famous example. The reasons why it failed included it being too low, so users felt insecure and vulnerable in it – not a good thing for a road vehicle. It could also be seen as possibly too soon for its time. Now electric bikes, scooters, chairs and mobility scooters are common daily sights. A little more discussion with potential users would have identified the issues and probably would have led to a differently shaped, taller, product which may have been more successful.

By having a marketing mindset, the way customers are spoken to resonates with them much more. They help drive the success of the company.

A brief overview of the marketing Ps.

Many people will have heard about the Marketing Ps. These are not complicated; indeed they merely define the breadth of areas that marketing impacts in a business.

It all started with 4 Ps: Product, Price, Place and Promotion. But then for services 3 extra Ps were added to give 7Ps: Physical evidence, People and Process.

These days of focus on Net Zero and Sustainability whenever the Author writes a marketing strategy for a client then she adds an 8th P: Planet. But often she also sums up the 7 Marketing Ps with a slightly modified (cleaner!) British Army saying:

Proper planning and preparation prevent pathetically poor performance.

Now isn't that what all businesses want to avoid? No-one wants poor performance. The marketing Ps as defined by the marketing gurus merely help with avoiding that poor performance.

What do all the Ps mean in brief?

Product

What it is that you are selling; the product(s) or service(s) that your company offers the clients.

Sometimes reducing a product range can increase sales as confusion is removed. Back in 2000 a psychology experiment (Columbia and Stanford University) was conducted with one display table at a food market had 24 different types of jam, another on a different day had 6 different jams. Which table sold the most units? The 6 different jams. Less choice meant more sales. [9]

Sometimes customers don't want or need the amount of choices we think they do. Having less can be more, whether training courses or pairs of trousers, you can reduce your production costs and increase sales.

---

[9] https://hbr.org/2006/06/more-isnt-always-better

Before you launch a product, research to see if it is needed or wanted by your target audience. The examples of successful products being developed in error are few and far between. A 3M scientist was working on a strong adhesive back in the late 1960s. He failed as his formula gave a light glue that could be easily peeled and repositioned. To start off with it was a typical solution without a problem. Move to the mid-1970s Post-it notes were born, but they were not successful at first, they had to be given away for free for people to realise that they solved a problem that they did not know they had.[10]

Price

Rather obviously this is how much does your product or service cost.

This can depend on who your target audience is – there are hairdressers who do a wash and blow dry for £15, there are others who will charge over £150 for the same thing.

You can buy an electric Citroen Ami for a list price of £8,495 (price correct February 2024)[11], but you will only have a top speed of 28mph and a 46mile range. Or you can buy an electric Tesla Model X at £101,390 with a top speed of 155mph and a 358-mile range. (price taken from tesla.com February 2024). They are both cars. They are aimed at very different audiences.

Then there is using price as an integral part of your brand. For example, Aldi and Lidl use price as

---

[10] https://en.wikipedia.org/wiki/Post-it_Note

[11] https://www.citroen.co.uk/ami?gad_source=1&gclid=EAIaIQobChMIpLnDwZurhAMVxZxQBh3AwQuREAAYASAAEgLCo_D_BwE&gclsrc=aw.ds

their differentiator. They have been so successful at that they are now price matched by Sainsburys and Tesco. Who would have thought that Morrisons would be in the top three most expensive supermarkets in the UK five years ago? [12]

Price for business to consumer businesses is also being used as part of supporting their customers during the cost-of-living crisis. Primark have announced that they will not increase prices in their new financial year despite having issues with currency rates and supplier increases.[13]

Of course, companies such as Primark, part of the huge ABT Group, have deeper pockets than many. They are looking at keeping customers loyal, as well as acquiring new customers who are moving down from the higher placed brands. The PR announcement for their "support" achieved such coverage that it was far more effective than an advertising campaign for raising awareness.

Place

This is the P that is most often misunderstood.

It is not necessarily the geographical location of your business, but it is always how you go to market.

Now for some service business, think a dry-cleaners or an independent furniture store, then the place is more likely to be fixed. Even if a home

---

[12] https://www.which.co.uk/reviews/supermarkets/article/supermarket-price-comparison-aPpYp9j1MFin

[13] https://news.sky.com/story/primark-will-not-increase-prices-further-as-sales-reach-pre-covid-levels-12741384

delivery / collection service is offered, then there will be a certain radius from the base.

For business-to-business companies, it may be that they only sell in the UK, or the UK and the EU. It may be that they are moving into export for the first time (imports may be more expensive when the pound is weak, but conversely exports are more cost-effective overseas).

For other companies, it is the route to market.

Do you sell direct via an e-commerce site, your own or Amazon / eBay / Etsy sites or your own shop / restaurant?

Do you sell through retailers or distributors? These could also include services such as Just Eat.

In the business-to-business IT space it is common for there to be 2 or 3 tiers:

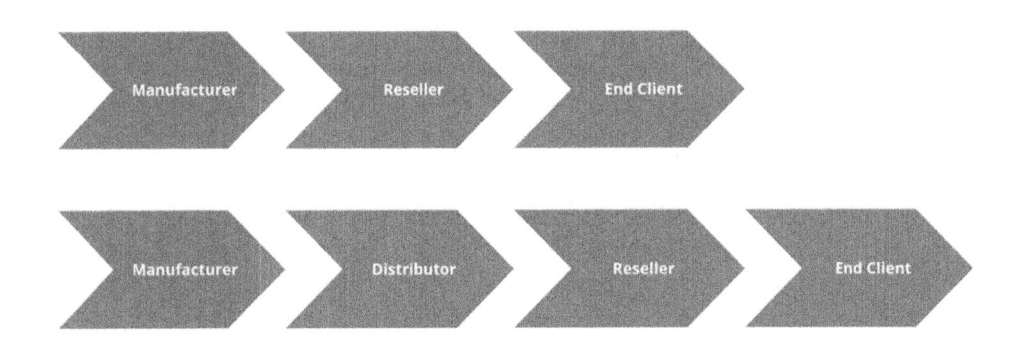

Manufacturer → Reseller → End Client

Manufacturer → Distributor → Reseller → End Client

Figure 2: 2 and 3 tier IT channels

If exporting, then there may be an import agent to add to the chain.

Some companies combine selling directly with selling through a channel. This has to be handled carefully so that your resellers trust you.

Promotion

How you tell your target audience about your product or service?

This is where the idea marketing is advertising comes from. There are many methods of spreading your message though that are not display advertising or Google Ads.

This is an area that we will go into detail on in the coming pages.

Physical Evidence

If you are a service business, then it may be that you give an appointment card that is branded up. It could be the way that your restaurant is branded and laid out. You recognise being in a TGI Fridays by the décor even if you didn't notice the brand on the way in. Uniforms also fall under this category. Seeing orange and purple at the supermarket you're in Sainsburys, green Asda, blue and red Tesco's.

Don't underestimated the importance of this part of marketing for your overall brand awareness.

People

Everyone in a service business or any customer interacting individual in a product business have an impact on how the customer perceives the experience.

Think about the impact of having a bad call centre experience when phoning to find a lost parcel means next time instead of Evri then another carrier will be used.

The author was once told by a Tesco Customer Services person that they didn't need her business when a 3 for 2 offer was not honoured at the checkout. Fast forward 20 or so years and the author still avoids Tesco as a result – what is the cost of that in terms of lifetime value?

However, having a member of staff who is trained and polite, goes that extra mile if needed, means that you are more likely to be recommended.

Process

The P that gets overlooked more than any other. Process is key in marketing though.

Processes are not just the remit of the Operations, Logistics or IT departments to sort out.

Marketing should define what the ideal process looks like to maximise return purchases, customer satisfaction and increased share of wallet. Whether that is the ecommerce web journey to basket and checkout, or the booking process at an exclusive restaurant.

Spending time developing the processes for the optimum experience can uncover gaps, increase sales and can also help to reduce costs to increase profitability.

Planet

In these days of Net Zero targets and customers who are looking for sustainability from their suppliers, then Planet is becoming ever more important.

NEVER greenwash – you will be called out for it, and it will have a negative impact on your brand. Indeed in the UK the Advertising Standards Authority (ASA) is now banning adverts which make environmental statements that can not be backed up by evidence. The Green Claims Code underpins this.[14]

Look at sustainability measures that have a positive impact on your business bottom line and then let clients know. Ask your clients what they expect to see from you in terms of planet.

Work up an ESG (Environmental, Social, Governance) strategy and place it on your website for accountability.

Small things can make a big difference and are noticed by customers: recycled serviettes in your pub, refillable metal soap holders in your toilets instead of single use bottles of handwash, LED lighting throughout your offices, automatic blinds that keep out the solar gain in the summer to reduce air conditioning without productivity dropping because it is too hot. If you can achieve BCorp certification that is absolutely fantastic. Take a free of charge B Impact Assessment[15] so that you identify areas that you need to look at. Or look at obtaining ISO14001.[16]

Being a good corporate citizen, supporting your customers, your supply chain and the environment, all foster loyalty and give a positive brand impact. When it comes down to it much of marketing strategy is good common sense business strategy too.

---

[14] https://www.gov.uk/government/publications/green-claims-code-making-environmental-claims

[15] https://www.bcorporation.net/en-us/programs-and-tools/b-impact-assessment/

[16] https://www.iso.org/standard/60857.html

I don't want all those Ps. How else can I define Marketing?

You can also think of the 6 Ws:

What, Who, Where, When, Why, How

Let's go through each in turn:

What

This is your product or service that you are selling.

Who

Your ideal client, customer or user. Do they have specific demographics, for example, are you aiming at females aged 18 – 30, or the over 60s?

Do they live in a certain geography, whether a town, city, county, state, country or continent?

Do they belong to a certain social strata or income level?

Do they have a specific job role / job title?

Do they have a certain level of education?

Do they have a specific interest / hobby that fits your product or service.

The more you understand who you are targeting then the more cost effective your marketing will be, and you will see higher returns on investment.

We will be talking about defining your ideal customer in more detail later on.

Where

Where you are selling your product or service and how you are going to market.

If you have a new toy you are launching you may decide to sell directly via your own e-commerce shop, or via a platform such as Etsy or eBay, you may decide to sell via retailers to increase the sales volumes.

If you are a B2B company, you may decide to reward partners and affiliates with a referral fee if they pass a lead to you that converts to a sale.

This is of course the same as the Place in the Ps.

Different routes to market will require different marketing collaterals to support them effectively.

When

Is your product or service seasonal? Is it something that can be sold all year round. For example, if you are an agency for models and actors who has a specialism in Father Christmas and Elves, amongst others, then marketing the Christmas themed solutions in February is going to be a waste of time.

For some other businesses then the seasons may be counter intuitive. For example, many B2B marketing agencies are the busiest in August in Europe. Why? Because before their clients entered the summer holiday season, they decided on various marketing campaigns that they want to launch in September when the end users are back from vacation. During August the agencies are busy finalising the campaigns ready for that September launch.

If your product is not seasonal, you may still see variations during the year that you may want to support with marketing activity.

In some cases, companies withdraw a product from sale and reintroduce with a fanfare later in the year. For example, in Mediterranean countries Ferrero Rocher are recalled in the summer when temperatures rise.[17] Instead Ferrero promotes the Raffaello product, as it doesn't melt as the chocolate does. So, their brand image is not affected from a messy melted chocolate experience. In 2023, they have extended their product offering with Ferrero Rocher and Raffaello ice-creams (but the advertising is as bad as the Ambassador you are spoiling us adverts that we all remember).

Also, some events may impact. Black Friday and Cyber Monday have been exported from the US to other countries. You may decide that you want to have a promotional activity at that time to benefit from the Black Friday hype, but you may also find it difficult to have your voice heard in the noise so decide to have your offer at another time of year.

Why

As any parent will tell you a young child will go through the phase of asking why, why, why, why. It is the most difficult question to ask with a response that answers it fully.

It is the same in Marketing.

The why question should be multi-layered and cascade as demonstrated below.

---

[17] https://www.dailymail.co.uk/news/article-3311559/The-real-life-Willy-Wonka-world-s-richest-chocolatier-invented-Ferrero-Rocher-Nutella-Kinder-hid-secret-recipes-Arabic-Cairo-away-spies.html

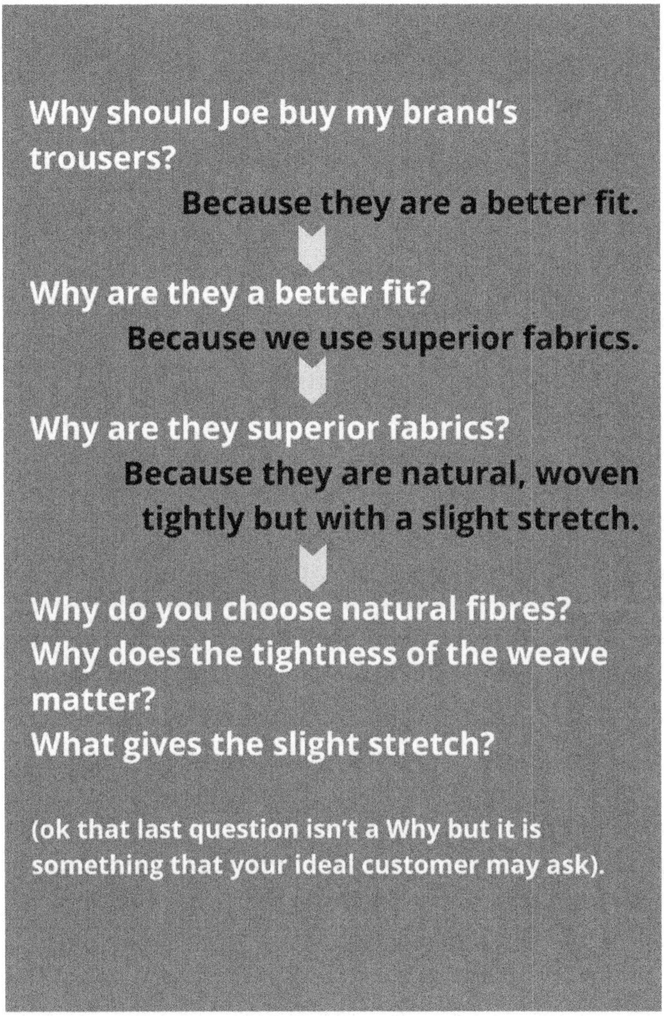

> **Why should Joe buy my brand's trousers?**
>   **Because they are a better fit.**
>
> **Why are they a better fit?**
>   **Because we use superior fabrics.**
>
> **Why are they superior fabrics?**
>   **Because they are natural, woven tightly but with a slight stretch.**
>
> **Why do you choose natural fibres?**
> **Why does the tightness of the weave matter?**
> **What gives the slight stretch?**
>
> (ok that last question isn't a Why but it is something that your ideal customer may ask).

Figure 3: An Example Why Cascade

You see what is meant by multi-layered.

The why answers why your product or service is the best fit for your ideal customer.

The why explains what is unique about your offering and why it should be chosen over other offerings.

Sometimes you will see this referred to as the unique selling proposition (USP).

How

There are two elements here. Firstly, how are you going to let your ideal customers know that your product is available? What forms of marketing are you going to use?

Secondly, how is your product or service going to be of use to your customer? How is it going to improve their life? How is going to make their jobs easier?

These are very closely related to the whys.

Summary

As we can see, much of the Ps and Ws really affects the business overall. Being on top of them allows you to ensure your business is as strong as it can be.

Take your time and go through each one, then you will have a marketing led business. Companies who put marketing and the customer first tend to be very successful. Just think of companies such as Apple. Steve Jobs insisted that each iPod was fully charged before being packaged, so that the customer could have instant use of the product. Instant gratification from their purchase.

Defining your target audience

Make the customer the hero of your story

– Ann Handley

Do you truly know what your ideal customer looks like? What they think of your product or service? What key messages they need to see and where for them to act?

In the Who section above we gave a top-level look at defining your target audience. Looking at demographics, interests, what they may read, TV shows that they are interested in and so on.

The more that you understand your ideal customer the clearer the messaging will be. The more likely that it will attract your target. For example, in August 2023 KFC were running an advertising campaign on UK TV around a teriyaki burger. They were obviously targeting the digital natives, a younger demographic.

The adverts are headed up by GK Barry, an internet personality, social media influencer and presenter. She has her own YouTube channel with circa 350,000 subscribers and a TikTok following of over 3 million.

The author is not ashamed to say that she had to look up who GK Barry was. Obviously, not in the target demographic for that advert series.

By understanding the who we can build up different tribes or segments.

Here is an example of buyer persona definition matrix for a business to consumer audience. Don't be scared of naming your individual buyer personas – it saves time in meetings, and it really brings that person to life, so you are talking to them not a faceless individual.

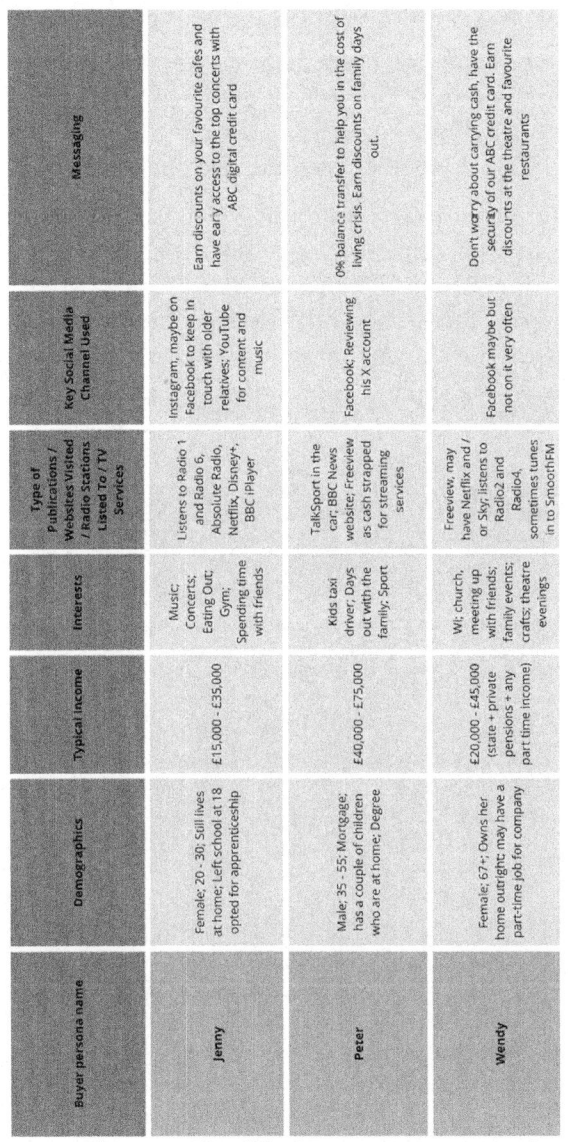

Buyer persona name	Demographics	Typical income	Interests	Type of Publications / Websites Visited / Radio Stations Listed To / TV Services	Key Social Media Channel Used	Messaging
Jenny	Female; 20 - 30; Still lives at home; Left school at 18 opted for apprenticeship	£15,000 - £35,000	Music; Concerts; Eating Out; Gym; Spending time with friends	Listens to Radio 1 and Radio 6, Absolute Radio, Netflix, Disney+, BBC iPlayer	Instagram; maybe on Facebook to keep in touch with older relatives; YouTube for content and music	Earn discounts on your favourite cafes and have early access to the top concerts with ABC digital credit card
Peter	Male; 35 - 55; Mortgage; has a couple of children who are at home; Degree	£40,000 - £75,000	Kids taxi driver; Days out with the family; Sport	TalkSport in the car; BBC News website; Freeview as cash strapped for streaming services	Facebook: Reviewing his X account	0% balance transfer to help you in the cost of living crisis. Earn discounts on family days out.
Wendy	Female; 67+; Owns her home outright; may have a part-time job for company	£20,000 - £45,000 (state + private pensions + any part time income)	WI; church, meeting up with friends; family events; crafts; theatre evenings	Freeview, may have Netflix and / or Sky; listens to Radio2 and Radio4 sometimes tunes in to SmoothFM	Facebook maybe but not on it very often	Don't worry about carrying cash, have the security of our ABC credit card. Earn discounts at the theatre and favourite restaurants

Figure 4: Simplified Buyer Persona Matrix

Defining your audience is slightly more complex in one way in a business-to-business setting than in the business-to-consumer.

First of all, is your product or service aimed at one particular vertical market. A vertical market is just another way of saying a market sector. For example, finance, public sector, healthcare, agriculture and so on.

Or is your product or service valid across multiple vertical markets as it is used in a frequently found department. These are often described as horizontal markets as they cross verticals. Think of accounting software, stationery, office chairs, laptops as a few examples. The sector the end client is in doesn't make a difference.

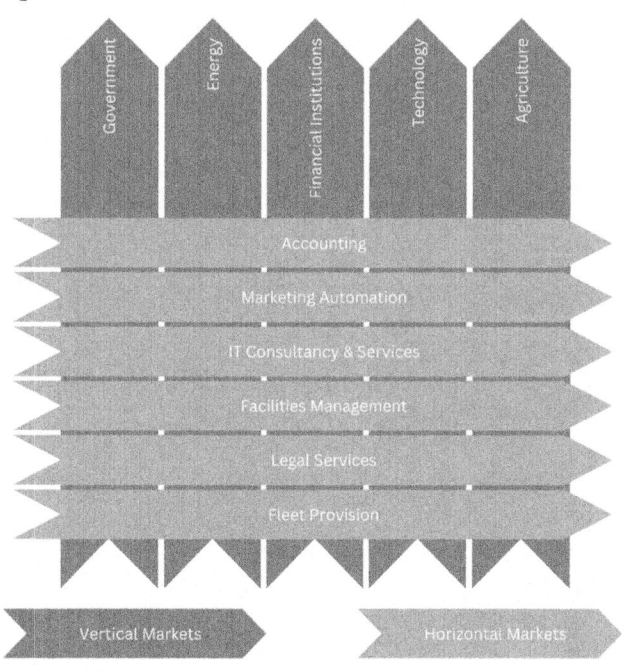

Figure 5: Vertical Markets and Horizontal Markets

Then, often in the business-to-business sector there are multiple people involved in the decision-making process. Different people will have different roles to play in the process. Here is an overview of those roles:

DMU elements / persona development

Technical Advisor

A key part of the decision-making unit for any company. This role will be looking at how the product or services fits with their needs, their current systems, their compliance requirements and any local regulations. They will be interested in how the product or service works to their benefit. How does it make their job easier? What are the reviews like on the internet? What are the case studies like – anything in their industry which means that they are not going out on a limb or taking a risk at the cutting edge of the technology / process / industry?

Buyer

Some organisations do not have a buyer per se, for example, trade finance does not go through a purchasing department.

However, for the majority of the companies out there there is a person who is responsible for purchasing. In many companies the purchasing person / team / department will run a series of Preferred Suppliers' Lists (PSL). These are companies who have been pre-selected by the purchaser to make their jobs easier and quicker for regularly purchased items from stationery, to recruitment agencies, to IT suppliers and so on.

If your offering is likely to be on a PSL then you need to take steps to ensure that you are on that list.

Often buyers see their raison d'etre to be to reduce the cost of everything. They will try to negotiate a discount, longer payment terms, avoid pre-payments and so on. Work to get the purchaser on side. If you are offering a solution that means that there is only one company that is going to be invoicing instead of multiple companies – then you have just made their job easier. If you are BCorp or ISO14001 certified, then again you are making it easier for them to hit the ESG targets that they have been given.

Questions that they typically need answering include How are you going to make my job easier? Are you on my PSL, should you be on my PSL? What is the advantage of working with you instead of the incumbent? Will this company help with our ESG SLAs (service level agreements)?

Users

If you are providing new software to automate certain tasks, then you need to be aware of how users will be impacted. If part of their role is to be removed from them, what does that mean for them? Are they going to be empowered? Are they going to be trained in higher skilled activities which will lead to salary increases?

If you are providing a new piece of equipment, how ergonomic is it? Will it improve safety? Will it make their jobs easier? Will it prevent injury from repetitive actions?

Encourage the users to be part of the decision. If they have concerns and raise to a union, then demonstrate to the union why your offering is of benefit to their members.

Questions that they typically need replies to: Why can't we just do it as we've always done it? If this reduces the time to do the job, what happens to me and my co-workers in my team? Is my job at risk? How much training will we need? How transferable are these new skills? How will my salary be affected?

Budget Holder

In many companies this will be a department head CMO, Marketing Director, CHRO, HR Director, CIO, IT Director, CFO, Finance Director – who get the decision. In small companies it may be the MD or CEO who controls all spend.

Whatever their job title, the budget holder needs to know that the company is getting the best bang for the buck. That will vary depending on your offering, for example, if you are an events agency, then it will come down to how many attendees you can ensure will participate, that the sponsorship slots are sold and that your costs are competitive for the results delivered. However, if you are selling in a new software package, then it will be about the total cost of ownership, what the payback cycle is.

This role needs to hear about return on investment. What the advantage is of spending the money with you instead of someone else. That they are getting the best value. That the overall spend will be lower.

For example, when the author bought her laptop, she spent £200 more for a higher specification, knowing that instead of a 3-year refresh cycle she could have a 5 year, possibly more, refresh cycle. So, in a 10-year period, instead of spending 3 x £1100 = £3300, the outlay would be 2 x £1300 = £2600. At first glance a £700 saving, but there is also the set-up time in having a new laptop, plus that annoying time spent getting used to the slightly different keyboard layout (why can't keys such as Home, End, Insert, Delete always be in the same place?). In addition, there is the time spent reviewing the latest models, finding the best place to buy from and processing the purchase.

All-in-all the savings are probably at least double the £700. At first glance a saving of £1400 over 10 years does not sound a lot. But that is with one laptop. If you have 10 staff it is £14,000, 100 staff £140,000.

Put messages together that show the real value that you are bringing instead of selling merely on price.

The Gatekeeper

We have all come across this individual. This person may be a receptionist, maybe a PA, maybe someone else. They have the role to filter out "noise" from reaching the other members of the DMU.

They need to be convinced so that they (a) allow the messages (whether email, direct mail, phone call or whatever) through or (b) raise the idea of your offering themselves as they see the value.

For many companies it is sending the message out in a way that the gatekeeper can not stop. Maybe a quick conversation at an industry event to book in a longer chat. A case study read in a relevant publication. It may even be a radio advert on Talk Sport as they drive to the office.

For the Gatekeeper themselves, for them to allow the communication through or even recommend it themselves, then they need to see the answer to the various questions under the other roles. Never make the mistake of thinking that they are "just" the receptionist or "just" the PA – these people can make and break many an introduction to a company. Treat them with respect and your job will be easier.

The Initiator

The person who realises that your type of offering is required. They start the whole process into looking into the need. If you are running a translation agency, this person may be a marketing executive tasked with localising documentation into various languages. If you are offering cybersecurity solutions then this person may be an IT Manager or a Compliance Officer.

They can be one of the above groups or someone completely different.

For this person you really need to answer the what's in it for me question. How is this going to help me do my job? How is it going to make my life easier? Is this a company that I can work with?

Decision Maker

Once again, this person may be one of the above groups or someone outside the group.

They are the ultimate decision maker. They take input from everyone else in the decision-making unit and then they decide to agree or override.

Many readers will have worked with a boss who just decided that something had to be purchased or done because (s)he said so. Many readers will also have worked with a boss who was the exact opposite and put pay to a good idea.

That latter point also applies to headquarters. It could be that the London office thinks that something is a good idea. They then present it to the HQ in New York who also think it is a good idea, but somehow it then gets lost in the whole HQ process.

Be careful to identify the true decision maker as soon as possible in the process. You don't want to be in a situation where you do a lot of work, and then find out that the global contract goes elsewhere as you missed out a key player in the decision-making team.

Thrive, Not Just Survive

Crafting Your Unique Selling Proposition (USP)

"The USP is the nucleus around which you build your success, fame, and wealth."

- Jay Abraham

Having a USP or a clearly defined value proposition sounds like marketing jargon, doesn't it? Well in many ways it is.

Let's demystify it.

Simply put your USP is what makes you different from everyone else out there. It is why you should work with supplier ABC over supplier XYZ. It is the thing that means that they are the must have company to work with.

Your USP should not be price – price wars benefit no-one in the long run.

Your USP should be a piece of value that you give that has meaningful impact for your target clients. Do not think of product or solution features, instead think of the benefits that those features give. The table below has a few EV vehicle features and the benefits they translate into for the drivers.

EV Feature	Benefit 1	Benefit 2	Benefit 3	Benefit 4
500 mile range	Less time charging, more time driving	Charge up at home and don't have to worry about recharging	Maximise use of at home solar panel generated electricity for free driving	Avoid spending those coffees and cakes whilst recharging when out
9 airbags	In the event of an accident more likely to walk away	Knee airbags removes the risk of feet being caught under pedals (thus avoiding in vehicle amputations)	Lower insurance premiums	
Apple Play	Full contact book available without having to sync regularly	Pick up where you left off in your audio book as you travel	Have multiple sat navs available - in car, Waze, Google Maps	Have your full music library available

Table 1: Feature Benefit Table Example

The author has mentioned the term What's In It For Me? (WIIFM) that is what you need to have in your USPs and value proposition. Your value proposition is simply the answer to the WIIFM question.

These are the reasons that your firm is chosen over another one. For example, if you are digital marketing agency, then there are many of those around. So what, sets you apart from the crowd.

Been around since 2010 – so longevity, trustworthy is implicit otherwise the company would not still exist. Early adopter of the social media platforms, so you have the knowledge of getting the most out of them.

Client list – which companies have you worked with. Are there any that are complimentary to your prospect's firm, any in the same sector so that knowledge is already there, and learning curves are reduced so that your clients get their results more quickly. Is your company used to working with companies of the prospect's size? Would they be a small fish in a big pond so not necessarily getting the support that they would expect (or need)? Would they be a very big fish in a small pond, such that the agency is over reliant on them as a client; that the client pulls resources away from other clients to their detriment?

Technological fit – do you offer to work with the tools and that prospect is already working with. Do you insist that everyone works on a certain platform for your ease? (Yes there are companies out there that do this)

Creativity skills – have you got in house photographers, graphic artists, videographers? After all imagery is absolutely necessary to catch eyeballs.

Results – list down provable results that have been achieved for other clients. That way you are removing the fear of trusting you.

Systems – how you make the approval process easy for the client so that they are not spending as much time on approving as if they were to generate the content themselves.

The list can quite easily go on. For different clients, for different types of buyers then the elements of the value proposition pulled out for each will differ.

A clear value proposition will match your firm's features, benefits and experiences to your clients wants, and needs whilst removing their fears.

In the B2B space, very often it is about showing why your solution is the pain relief to your client's headache. Very often they do not care about the ingredients in the pain relief, they just want to be able to know and trust that it will deliver as expected.

There is a common example given. You have a raging toothache. You are on the way to a very important meeting, and you just want the pain to be gone. You dash into a chemist. On the shelf you see all types of pain relievers. One says this cures tooth ache in 2 minutes – that is the one you grab and take to the till with a bottle of water to swill it down. Two minutes later job done. Meeting held successfully.

You don't consider the ingredients. You don't consider the price. You consider the product promise and the value you place on that product promise in your selection.

That is what your value proposition needs to set out clearly.

When you draft it, test it on other staff, test it on current clients. Then test it in the marketplace.

Setting SMART Marketing Goals: Creating measurable and achievable marketing objectives.

"If you don't know where you are going, you will probably end up somewhere else."

– Lawrence J. Peter

In turbulent times you want to ensure that every penny spent on marketing has its returns. You will want to keep an eye on expected returns and actual returns.

One of the easiest ways to do this is to set SMART goals. Here we will go through what each letter in the SMART system means.

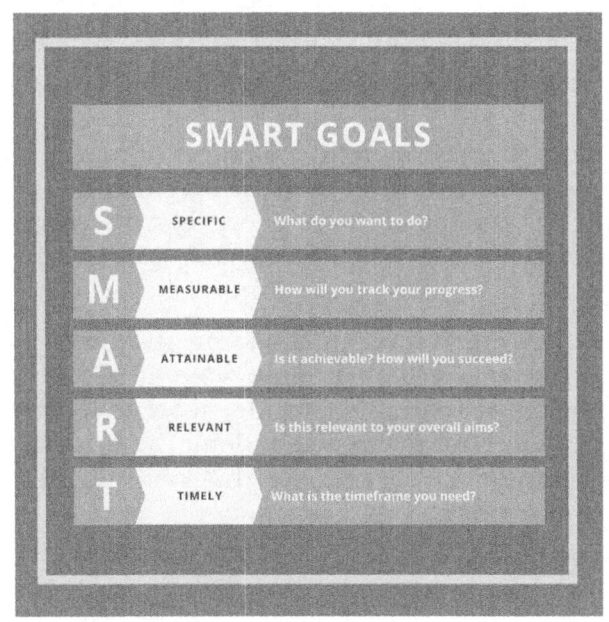

Figure 6: SMART Goal Definitions

Let's start with S: Specific

Your goal should be precise. The more precise the better. It is always better to have two or three more exact goals than one that is so generic that it could mean anything.

For example, instead of "bring in new customers", for the marketing campaign that you are looking at, what type of new customers?

Use "To sign-up new clients that turnover at least £500,000 in the care home sector".

You may think that that is still rather generic, but as we move through the SMART mnemonic it will get steadily more and more detailed.

Moving to M: Measurable

You want to have new clients, but how many clients? What financial impact would that have on your organisation at the typical spend? It may be absolute terms, or it may be in percentage terms.

For example, instead of saying "increase sales" say "increase sales by £10,000 or 10%". You may want to quantify how that compares to the overall market. So you may say that you want to grow revenue by 15% in a market growing at 10% year on year. So you are outperforming the market. You are not just taking inflationary growth and seeing that as a success.

There is nothing wrong with having stretch targets, but targets must be achievable. If you set targets that are reaching for Jupiter instead of the Moon, then you could very easily demotivate your team. Why would they try to give their all if it still won't be good enough?

So yes, the goals need to be A: Attainable. You may have an aggressive target, but then temper it with another couple of goals that would still be successful and drive the company forwards.

For example, if you are running a campaign to increase sales and / or market share, then you may have other targets that are on softer targets: number of case studies achieved through the campaign; number of new opt-in names on your database; increase in engagements on your social media; amount of coverage on industry news / partner websites about your campaign.

The next element is R: Relevant.

There is no good having a goal if it is not moving the business in the overall direction wanted. It has to fit with the business objectives. The market and its conditions (don't try to sell heating systems in the middle of a heatwave, instead prioritise air conditioning units).

If your business doesn't have detailed goals for the next 1, 3, 5 years, then you need to put them into place, and again they need to be SMART. The marketing goals can then flow from them.

It staggers the Author the number of times she asks her consultancy clients what does success look like in 1, 3, 5 years' time and the CEO sitting opposite her says "I don't know". Know what you are aiming for to drive your business forwards.

Goals can change. During the 21st century we have seen clearly how goals have had to change due to financial crashes and pandemics. But you should always have goals in place so that you can recognise when and where you need to pivot and change plans.

The final letter is T for timely.

Each goal should say over what timeframe it is going to be measured.

To expand out the example above for the care home campaign:

To sign-up 5 new clients that turnover at least £500,000 in the care home sector leading to a 10% increase in revenue compared to last year and 12% increase in net profit within the next 12 months.

To increase the number of engagements on our social media posts by 125% in the next 12 months.

To secure 2 new case studies from the new clients.

To achieve coverage in 10 key industry publications over the course of the 12 months. (you could even name the publications if you wish)

You can see that the goals are all very exact, but at the same time achievable. They fit with the company's objective to grow by 25% over the next 3 years.

SMART Goal setting is an art and a science, like a lot of marketing. It will help to focus the mind and the spend. In the above example, a lot of that may be done in house with little additional spend apart from time dedicated to the social media authoring, the PR and case study writing.

It may be that during the campaign, sales enablement tools are uncovered that increase conversion rates. There doesn't need to be a lot of money spent.

Section II: Marketing in Turbulent Times

"If you want creativity, take a zero off your budget. If you want sustainability take off two zeros."
- Jaime Lerner

In the previous section we laid the foundations from knowing who your customers are to setting objectives, now we can start to discuss how to get those messages out there.

Be honest, this is the part of the book that you thought you needed the most.

Which marketing communications tools will help you not just survive but also grow and thrive during this turbulent time? Even if your marketing budget is zero, there are still things that you can do.

It will be a combination of things, no one tool will be a cure all, because your prospects all have their preferences of where and how they consume messages too.

Communication Flows

"Nothing in life is more important than the ability to communicate effectively."

– Gerald R. Ford, former United States president

Whenever you send messaging out you should be aware of the audience, but in a B2B situation that may be more complex than you first think.

Here are some sample communication flows. In the first one, we are looking at an IT reseller, how the distributors and vendors communicate, along with how they interact with the end customer companies.

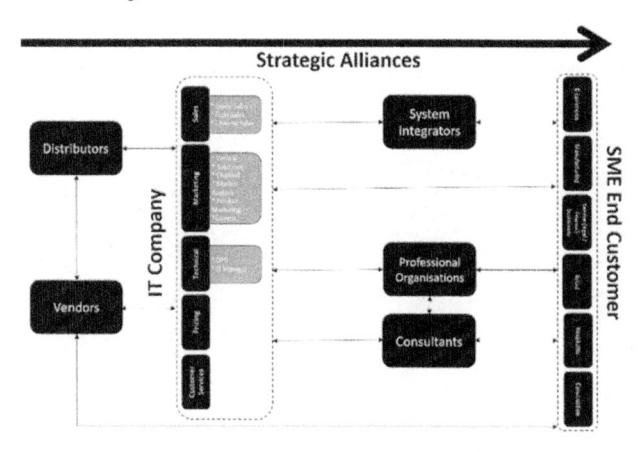

Figure 7: Sample Communication Flow for an IT Vendor

This next one shows a company targeting the healthcare sector in the UK. A lot more complicated, because of the complexity of the NHS on the public side, plus the private healthcare sector.

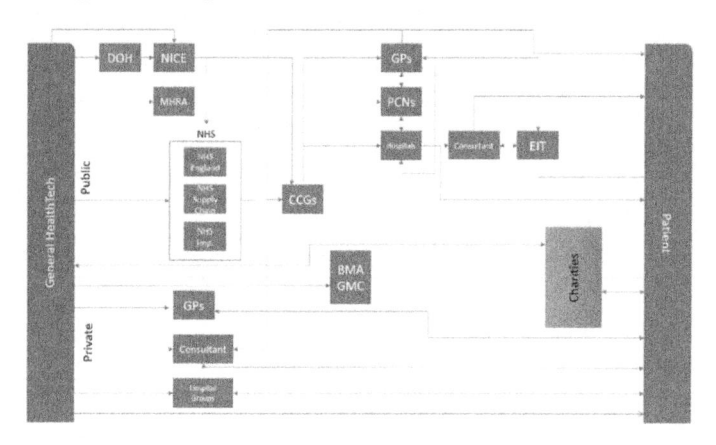

Figure 8: Communication Flows in UK Healthcare

As you can see the communication flows can vary enormously but these will help you identify the various routes your promotional messages need to follow.

Now we are going to go through the marketing communication tools.

Thrive, Not Just Survive

Social Media, Organic

"The best marketing doesn't feel like marketing."

– Tom Fishburne

There are a plethora of social media platforms out there. You should select one or two that are used by your target audience and do them well rather than try and be on all of them. Choose what not to do, is as important as choosing what you are going to do.

Social media can really help to reduce the variance in company budgets if used well. However, the organic algorithms can be skewed to individuals as opposed to businesses.

You need to ensure that you are having a conversation with your clients and prospects. Social media is not a broadcast media, any comments have to be read and responded to, that has a time overhead that has to be managed as the company grows.

The content does need to be tailored according to the platform, but in some cases the same content can be used across 2 or 3 of the platforms without too much degradation.

Organic social media is the posts that you issue free of charge. There is no fee for posting. So consider it to be editorial rather than advertising. The content should have a value for the audience and not just be a sales piece. Building the brand, thought leadership, credibility and gravitas as well as lead generation can all be achieved through organic social media.

If your clients decide that they want to use social media for Customer Services, it is not acceptable to tell them that they have to call or email. Courier company, Evri (used to be Hermes), has no social media accounts. That does not stop people complaining about them on social. All those methods will do is make the disappointed customers more vocal about the poor experience on social media.

The old adage used to be that a dissatisfied customer would tell between 9 and 15 people according to the White House Office of Consumer Affairs, now, with social media, that has been greatly amplified and your brand identity can be heavily impacted.

If the social algorithms are set to downplay business accounts in people's newsfeeds even if they have followed the business, how can businesses use their social media accounts to find new prospects?

First of all, don't fall into the trap that only the number of followers matters. Quantity is not the be all and end all. Instead, it is about quality of engagement with your business.

If your followers are liking, sharing or commenting then that will help your organic posts be more successful.

Encourage your staff and others to engage with your posts, especially in the first hour of being published. That way your posts will show up to their connections and followers too.

Use the full suite of tools. You may not feel too comfortable delivering a Facebook and / or LinkedIn Live, but it will enable clients to see and hear the real you. They build trust. No-one is expecting you to be as smooth as Clive Myrie reading the news. If you fluff words, own it and move on.

If reels get excellent engagement, then use them.

Video attracts attention – they don't need to be professionally done. If you have a smart phone (and don't we all?) then you can do a video. If you want something a little more professional and less shaky you can invest in a ring light on a tripod where your phone is clipped in the middle of the light so you've studio lighting for a fraction of the cost! Did you know that you can put a video behind your profile picture on LinkedIn to give a more detailed introduction?

Don't necessarily follow every fad. If your prospects are not using TikTok then neither should you for your business. Instead concentrate on where they are found. It is far better to do one or two platforms well and consistently, than attempt to do more and not achieve optimum participation.

Build relationships with other complementary companies on social media and support each other's efforts. For example, there are a variety of X (Twitter) hours, for example, where companies from a certain geographic region or segment share ideas, tips and tricks, as well as leads and referrals with each other.

For each platform, ensure that you use a tone and content that is applicable to that platform, otherwise your posts will be ignored.

Research the best hashtags for your campaign but use them sparingly. If you wish you can create a hashtag for your campaign. Do not use hashtags in the body of the main post – they just make it more difficult to read – instead put them at the end. If you have used a term in the post, then there is no point in repeating it at the end. The searches will find the post anyway.

Don't forget to use the analysis tools – which posts have had most engagement. Is there something that you can replicate on future posts. Take the learnings and implement them.

There are whole books written about the social media platforms and how to use them. This book offers an overview for you to decide if they are appropriate for you as part of your marketing communications mix.

LinkedIn

For many B2B companies, the main platform to build credibility and gravitas as well as partnerships with affiliates and funders will be LinkedIn.

With LinkedIn the consistency of posting is key. If you start to post every day, and then stop for a while, when you restart then the reach will be negatively impacted. Start with a posting schedule that you can maintain. Not only will it give you favours with the algorithm, but your followers will know when to expect your content.

Post format should vary: text + image, carousel, video snippet, poll. Different formats have different levels of support from LinkedIn – videos have been downplayed more recently by the LinkedIn algorithm, but they are still more likely to be shown to your followers then text only or text + image.

Polls were prioritised by LinkedIn but there is some anecdotal evidence that since the start of 2023 the reach of polls has been downgraded a little. This has probably been due to the introduction of the document post, also known as a carousel.

Carousels are easy to do. The content needs more planning but can be an eye-catching way to get a longer message out there, or even use to tease a message out. Just upload a PDF, preferably in a square format, and LinkedIn will do the rest.

Thrive, Not Just Survive

By using a variety of post types, it is more likely to encourage engagement as different people have different preferences. Once someone engages once with a post then future posts are more likely to appear in their feed too.

For new followers on LinkedIn, they see the posts for the first week or two of following. That is the window of opportunity to encourage them to engage with quality content so that the posts are seen in the future.

Company page reach is always lower than individual posts. That flows nicely into the next point, the first 90 minutes of any post going live determines how much reach it will achieve. The LinkedIn algorithm rewards posts that have comments, reposts and likes by showing them to more of the company's followers. The weighting is in the order stated, so encourage staff to comment or repost before they like the post and preferably in that first 90minutes if practical.

Any comments received in that first 90 minutes should also be responded to pretty much straight away. It encourages dialogue, shows that social media is being used for social networking and not just broadcast, plus increases the number of comments pushing the reach up further.

Live posting in LinkedIn is also given priority to the feeds over using schedulers such as Buffer, Hootsuite or even LinkedIn's own scheduler. LinkedIn is a commercial beast – if posting live then you are on the site seeing the adverts. Nothing more complicated than that.

If your company page has more than 150 followers, then you will have access to creator mode. You will need to switch creator mode on, which encourages LinkedIn to feature your page on nonfollowers' streams to spread your message further. In addition, you will have access to some advanced features including:

LinkedIn Lives (proactively promoted by LinkedIn to people they think will be interested). A cost-effective way of hosting a webinar. To host a LinkedIn Live a third-party piece of software is needed. The one the author uses is StreamYard, simple to use, costs circa $20 a month if editable videos are needed (recommended as gives content for the future) and allows for your own branding. Other equipment needed – a good quality Lavelle microphone, a ring light for professional looking lighting (or if you wear specs then consider a small LED panel off to the side and above instead and turn down the brightness on your own screen so that the reflections are minimised) and if using a virtual backdrop a green screen. All that equipment can be procured from Amazon at a total cost below £150 inc VAT.

LinkedIn Newsletters: These can be weekly, fortnightly or monthly. The advantages are that the first edition is automatically sent to all followers. The second edition is then sent to newsletter subscribers. In addition, when sent out it is sent as a notification in LinkedIn itself as well as an email. GDPR issues are avoided. Further, no special software is required. The disadvantages are that it is fairly basic in layout offerings – one column for example. The email addresses are not collated automatically for the subscribers, but a list of subscribers is visible on LinkedIn for cross-checking with your CRM system.

Additional analytics are available on combined posts and audience demographics.

To maximise reach hashtags are key on social media – including LinkedIn. They allow people who are not following your page to see the content in which they are interested.

Hashtag research should be completed by platform. To check the hashtag audience on LinkedIn type the hashtag into the search bar then click on the hashtag as it shows up. The audience size will then be shown.

Hashtags should be used with the largest audience first, then the second largest and then the third. Do not overuse hashtags as that reduces reach. Ideally, you should seek to use 3-4 hashtags on each post.

The below table shows examples of hashtags for a B2B marketing consultancy. Of course any hashtag list you generate would need checking every couple of months.

Hashtag	Size of audience on LinkedIn
#marketing	20,217,159
#marketingb2b	4,214
#b2bmarketing	41,106
#marketingstrategy	85,173
#marketingstrategies	3,327
#b2b	40,023
#startup	1,030,660
#startups	21,054,464
#sme	6,559
#smallbusiness	812,053
#smallbusinesses	4,278
#smallbiz	8,243
#smallbusinessmarketing	3,673
#startupmarketing	547
#technology	26,213,153
#tech	167,897

Table 2: Sample LinkedIn Hashtag Volumes

Note how small changes can change the audience size greatly. However, be aware of what your target audience is searching for and use what they use.

Whilst not everybody who follows the hashtags chosen will be interested in your message, that audience is a lot larger. As posts are downgraded for visibility if they have less than 3 or more than 4 hashtags, combining for coverage and topic is recommended.

Twitter / X / Threads / Mastodon

Just a few months ago, Twitter was the place to build relationships with journalists and bloggers for the benefit of the brand. Many companies built relationships through Twitter Hours.

Then Elon Musk arrived.

Twitter has become X. Users have plummeted. Blue ticks are now paid for. Some journalists and companies have left the platform as they do not like the way it is moving or how it could affect their brand image.

Meta launched Threads, however, to have an account you have to have an Instagram account first. The number of users increased rapidly in the first few days and has now fallen back a little.

Mastodon is also twitteresque in microblogging terms. However, it hasn't gained ground as quickly as Twitter has lost users. Many see Mastodon as complex, as it is distributed in nature. Different servers have different rules of what is permissible.

The future will be interesting in how this microblogging sector develops. Will X find its roots again? Will Threads become standalone? Will Mastodon continue its steady growth? Will another platform enter the frame?

Facebook / Instagram

Some B2B companies have great success with Facebook and / or Instagram, especially if they have a B2C offering too. Others have no success whatsoever.

If you are targeting smaller SMEs, then you may enjoy more success. If you want to build a community then one option is you do that through a Facebook group.

Many of the points that were discussed in the section about LinkedIn are true with these platforms too. Varying the types of posts used, researching hashtags, setting a consistent posting schedule.

If you wish to use Threads, then you will need a company Instagram account too.

Others: TikTok, Snapchat, Pinterest

TikTok has seen an increase in B2B participation. However, there are issues with TikTok and its Chinese ownership. Some Governments have banned TikTok, for example India back in 2020, more recently The US State of Montana is the first state to make it illegal for TikTok to be on personal devices[18]. That came into force in January 2024, although the fines will be for App Stores that allow access to TikTok as opposed to individuals themselves. That move follows a plethora of US states banning TikTok from public sector devices.[19]

This demonstrates how social media channels can come and go for a variety of reasons. Do any readers remember Friends Reunited, before it became a dating app? Or what about MySpace?

If your target audience is a younger demographic, then you may think about Snapchat. On a business-to-business side it has limited applicability.

Pinterest tends to be underutilised by B2B companies. There are opportunities there, if it

---

[18] https://www.techtarget.com/whatis/feature/TikTok-bans-explained-Everything-you-need-to-know

[19] https://www.nytimes.com/article/tiktok-ban.html

matches your audience base. It is more frequently used by B2C companies.

Social Media Paid For

> *"Marketing's job is never done. It's about perpetual motion. We must continue to innovate every day."*
>
> – Beth Comstock

Each of the social media platforms has to cover costs and be commercial in their own rights. Therefore, each platform offers various types of paid for activity.

Boosting posts in the past was just a way to increase the visibility to the current followers. But these days boosting posts on Facebook is a quick and easy way to use your current content as an advert. The audience can be defined down to your target and the minimum spend is 1USD a day.

The level of reporting has also improved greatly. You can really see if your boosting has improved your ROI.

If you want to use specific adverts, as opposed to using organic content in place of an advert, then Meta Ad Manager comes into play for Facebook, Instagram and WhatsApp.

Facebook, Instagram and X(Twitter) adverts can be targeted according to demography, geography, interests and so on, as well as having a company page where people can comment and follow for unique offers. You can set a budget split by day or number of click throughs.

Running an advertising campaign on LinkedIn is not for the feint hearted. It is a major investment since the algorithm changed last year to reward long term advertisers.

Now each time a campaign is started, each advert's LinkedIn rating is 1 (even if the same advert on a previous campaign had a rating of 20). As the campaign runs and there is engagement that rating increases as it is seen as being relevant. The price paid for the advert is determined by a combination of the rating and the bid amount.

If, as a new advertiser, you bid £10 for a slot, and a long running advertiser with a bid rating of 2 also bid for that slot to the same audience, but only bid £5, they would be given priority as 10 x 1 = 10 and 5 x 2 = 10 but rating is rewarded when a tie.

As a new advertiser then the recommendation coming from LinkedIn is to have a budget of at least £100 per day and to run for at least three months, if not continually. The minimum spend is $7 a day, but the 30-day budget should be 3 times that so $630. At $7 a day you may never be seen.

It can be seen that a lot of money can be committed before knowing the results.

That is a hefty ouch!

However, adverts can be tailored for the required result – impressions (not to be recommended as impressions is merely a vanity metric more of that in the next section of the book), click through to your landing page or lead generation, but each campaign can only have one of those. If a new advert is added to the campaign, it also starts on a rating of 1.

LinkedIn sometimes do offer a credit towards advertising spend as a marketing tool for themselves. If you are considering advertising on there then have a look around for one of those.

If LinkedIn advertising is to be added to the marketing mix, then detailed analysis as well as conversations with LinkedIn advertising department are recommended to evaluate whether display advertising or sponsored posts (advertorial) would be the better way to go for your company.

Where you place any advertising depends on where your target audience is active as to where you target any spend.

However, to be truly successful, you need to have credibility in the value of your company page first and foremost, as many prospects will check that out before clicking through. So, get the organic right first and foremost.

Reach out to the relevant advertising team to find out what is the most effective route for you to take given your budget.

Never be bullied by any advertising salesperson to spend more than you want to. They have targets to attain which may not be in harmony with your targets and budgets.

SEM

"Always be relevant, create relevant campaigns, and give the user the answer to his query as precisely as you can,"

- Marko Kvesic

Search Engine Marketing, whether Google Ads or on Bing, can be cost effective if concentrated on the correct terms (keywords). The more exact the term then the more cost effective.

One example the author has come across is a small company spending 4 figures on SEM each month with no return on investment. By looking into the keywords, then one term that they had not added into the campaign, raised its head.

The company were looking for 20 leads per month within a certain geography. The search term overlooked only had 80 searches per month, but it was for their service in their target geography. The term also had a low cost per click against it.

Spending a little time in research saved a lot of marketing spend – that is money that can go straight on the bottom line. What's not to like?

The advantage with SEM over standard display advertising is that the fee is only paid if the advert is clicked, and it is not based on a number of impressions. The cost per click(CPC) varies widely, determined by the term, but that the impression is free of charge.

Adverts need to be written to disqualify irrelevant clicks to reduce costs.

Very often if a business has not used Google Ads previously, they will offer a money off voucher, which is awarded if you spend a certain amount – sometimes it is £50 against a £50 spend, sometimes £400 voucher which is released once you have spent £400.

Don't forget with Google Ads you are only charged when someone clicks on your advert, but the advert being there still raises the brand awareness. A typical budget needed to make an impact is suggested by Google as you set up a campaign, but do not allow yourself to be "bullied" into spending more than you wish.

Bing also has SEM available – you decide where your customers are more likely to be searching to decide which is best for you.

Google have recently updated their Google Ads Management platform for small businesses to "make it easier". To date all the author has heard is complaints as it does not allow the granularity of term definition and gives Google more control over where the advert is placed. Costs have therefore increased with no equivalent increase in ROI. Using a Google Ads agency may pay for itself.

Another issue with SEM, as well as online display advertising, is the growth of ad blockers. Products such as Avast Business Security include an ad blocker as standard. Many companies are standardising on ad blockers to prevent accidental clicks to malware sites. The stats on ad blockers show a year-on-year rise across several research agencies, even if the percentages vary.

The growing prevalence of ad blockers may severely impact the reach of the adverts. Google is beginning to respond by showing some entries as "sponsored" as opposed to adverts, but the ad blockers will probably catch up with those too.

SEO

> *"Content is what the search engines use to fulfill user intent."*
>
> *- Dave Davies*

Search engine optimisation also uses keywords.

This time the terms are built into the content on the website, or as meta tags on the backend of the page.

By building those terms in a natural way into the web page content means more web traffic and organic leads instead of relying on SEM which has a cost per click.

Categories of long tail (the more exact search terms) keyword research include questions, comparisons, related searches. By using a tool such as Ubersuggest (which has similar functionality to SEMRush for a reduced fee) evaluate those that have an applicable search volume and preferably are easier for SEO ranking. In the snippet below a random search of strategic marketing consultancy in the UK brought back the following details:

A. From Strategic Marketing Consultancy there are 33 alternative keywords suggested
B. There is just 1 related keyword.
C. 16 questions
D. 9 prepositions
E. 11 comparisons

The term Strategic Marketing Consultancy has 320 searches per month with an average cost per click of £5.35 and a paid difficulty of 13/100 and a search difficulty of 33/100, making it relatively easy to rank on in paid terms, but more difficult for search. However, if you chose a "brand strategy consultancy London" there are 20 searches a month with an average price of £4.41 and a search difficulty of 9 – so much easier to have the links for free. Content should give you results easily without needing the spend.

Now if instead of strategic marketing consultancy we look at marketing consultancy.

A. 217 alternative keywords suggested
B. 599 related keywords
C. 28 questions
D. 14 prepositions
E. 21 comparisons

The term Marketing Consultancy is searched for 2900 times per month in the UK at an average cost per click of £3.00. Paid difficulty has risen to 24 and search difficulty to 35.

This time adding the word London to the search still gives 2900 searches per month and a cost per click of £4.63, a paid difficulty of 48/100 and a search difficulty of 42/100.

Sometimes the keywords will give ideas for white papers, blog articles, webinar topics and so on. So spending time on accurate keyword analysis can help with SEO, but also SEM and uncovering PR topics that are going to drive the business forward on topics that are currently being discussed.

To encourage the Google (and other search engine) spiders to visit the site, then SEO is going to be key, along with content that is updated on a regular basis – gone are the days of a website being a brochure online.

Thrive, Not Just Survive

You may hear of on page and off page SEO. On page is the content but also ensuring that the site is speedy to load, pictures have alternative text behind them, that the site is responsive, i.e. resizes to mobile easily and appropriately.

Off page SEO is when you receive back links to your site. As publications use your content then they may put a link to your site at the end too. If you have strategic partners, then the backlinks to the website should also increase which will help in SEO terms and rankings.

Don't just have them link to your homepage, but instead link to a specific, relevant page. Sometimes that is called a deep link.

Do not fall into the trap of paying someone for a certain number of backlinks. As backlinks are not all created equally. The higher the site's domain authority then the more valuable the back link.

For example, the domain authority of the BBC website is 95 according to Moz. It ranks for 519,000 keywords and has 1.8million linking root domains. That falls into the excellent category.

If you can work on your website to get it to a DA of 40-50 then it would be seen as average. Of course, it takes time to increase the domain authority. When your site has a higher domain authority it is more likely to appear on the first page of the search engine results – and that is where you want to be!

If you have a score of <30, then that is considered poor, 50-60 is classed as good, >60 is classed as excellent.

To increase the SEO results, separate pages per service or product set and sector are required. They can be tailored and used as landing pages thus increasing backlinks. Do not make the mistake of having all the content on one page, it will be downgraded by the spiders. However, from a content point of view the length should be at least 350 words, but for better results then 750 – 1500 words of quality content per page to really be optimal for the SEO spiders.

Nowhere should be more than 2-3 clicks from the homepage.

Google uses EEAT to rank content – Experience, Expertise, Authoritativeness, Trustworthiness. In your content use examples that show your experience, your expertise, quote sources and build trust. You may like to do a first draft using ChatGPT or Gemini, but then have a human go through it adding in things that are only known to your company.

Website

> *"Websites promote you 24/7: No employee will do that."*
>
> *– Paul Cookson*

It isn't necessarily true that you will need a website – some businesses are very successful without them relying on sales pages for specific campaigns or just not having one. But a website can be a very effective tool for expanding email lists, for having a central repository of PR pieces and so on.

At its very basic a website is a shop window visible to everyone. A brochure online. However, your site should be a living breathing entity not merely a brochure.

Keep the messaging clear for each of your target segments and ensure offerings are relevant to each. Keep your website content up to date and add content as and when relevant, for example, new blog posts or PR content, new white papers.

New content ensures repeat visitors. Valuable content increases dwell time on the site.

Your home page should be clear about what it is that you offer and who the target client is to avoid poor quality enquiries.

Have your mission statement, your vision statement, your company values displayed on your website along with your CSR (corporate social responsibility) and ESG (environmental social governance) aims for transparency and accountability.

Ensure that your website speaks to your target audience in terms that they recognise. Do not use jargon for jargon's sake, but at the same time, if you are a technology or pharmaceutical company, for example, then assumptions that the target audience have a certain level of knowledge can also be taken into account.

Content should answer the Why question – why does the company offer this, why is it valuable to the audience segment – more so than the how. You want to have replies to the issues faced by visitors and your company's paracetamol to the prospect's headache.

Each campaign should have a landing page or sales page that gives the campaign information plus has a call to action clearly defined. Google Analytics is your friend for seeing where the visits have come from, after all you want to track if it was organic search, Facebook, display advert on an industry website or somewhere else. You want to know where your money was best spent.

When you have a website then you need to ensure that the User Experience (UX) is what your prospects and customers would expect. That their journey through the site is as they expect, not as you think it should be!

If you start a blog on your site, then issue them regularly. That way you will build up a readership. Link to the blog articles from the social media platforms used. Don't be afraid to update and reissue blogs as life moves on. That can be an effective use of content, 90% is the same, 10% new – it all decreases the amount of work you have to do to keep that blog ticking over.

If time is a real consideration, then there are plenty of copywriters out there who will research and write SEO enabled blog posts for you. Paying them may be more cost effective than struggling to do it yourself.

Look for people who are specialist in your field. Ask to see samples of work. Give clear guidance re type of language to be used (casual, formal, professional, chatty) and the aims of the pieces.

Of course, you could also use tools such as ChatGPT, BUT you will have to check facts and double check that the content is unique, especially if you are in a crowded marketplace. Rarely can the content be used as is, but it can be a valuable first draft.

Consider a search function on the website to cover blogs / insights, PR pieces, white paper and case studies – often a simple tool to implement but will be powerful and allow content to be leveraged more easily in the sales funnel.

It can sound like a faff, but ensure that you have a unique, meaningful, short web address for each piece.

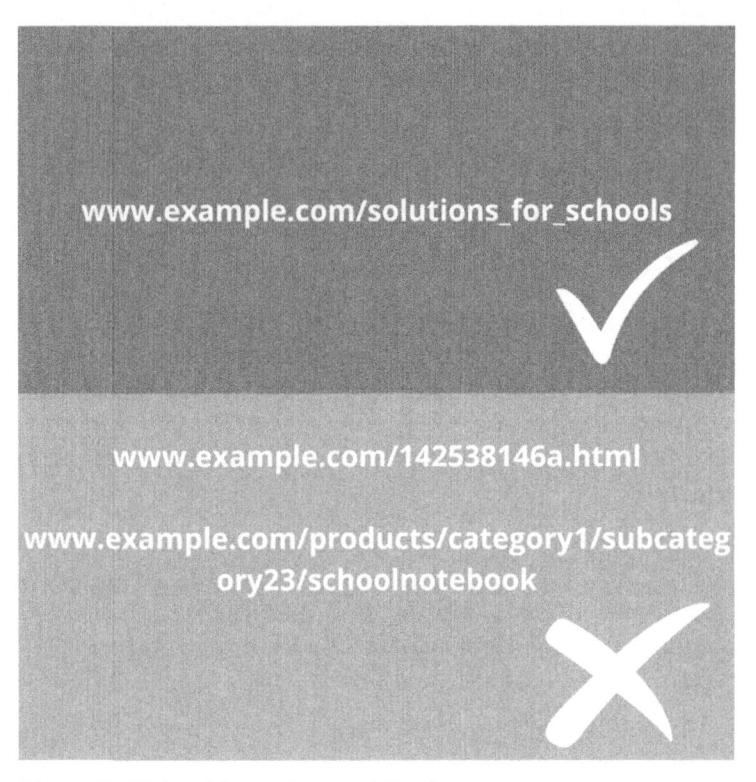

Figure 9: Web Address Dos and Don'ts

That helps the search engine spiders but also makes it easier to point people in the right direction from other communication methods, an email newsletter, a social post. Make it easy to remember and easy to type in.

Gated content, ie content that people have to enter an email address and name to be able to access, for email acquisition is something that comes in and out of fashion. As organic social media reach becomes ever more difficult for company pages, then building an opted-in email list is once again something that needs to be considered, despite the latest (February 2024) Gmail and Apple updates which can lock you out if you have more than 3 emails out of a thousand reported as spam.

Gated content is content deemed to be valuable enough for people to register an email address to be able to access it (and hopefully opt-in as well). Typically, white papers fall into this category when first uploaded to a website.

In addition, the data will be valuable to see who is downloading the white paper in terms of prospects, competitors, current or past clients, and which topics resonate the best.

If you do gate and are in the UK then make sure you are registered at the ICO, for many small companies it is £35 a year if paid by direct debit. More on that below in Email Marketing.

Sometimes, however, getting the content out is more important than the email addresses that could be captured. If a piece of content is to be a lead generator, then it needs to be read first and foremost. You do not want to make it difficult for the prospect to access it.

Consider carefully if gating content is the right thing for you to do. It may be that you gate it for a while when new and then open it up after a certain timeframe. Think Amazon Prime v Freevee, or seeing a movie on Sky Movies instead of waiting for the terrestrial channels to show it for free.

Intranets and extranets are terms that web designers will use when you are talking with them. Basically they are password protected areas of your website. Intranets are used for employees, especially in multi-location companies. Extranets are external groups.

An extranet may be an account area for customers to monitor orders and deliveries; if you sell through a two- or three-tiered channel then it may be a partner portal for resellers where they can download imagery or specific marketing content for them; or for investors where they can see the share price or an annual report.

Email marketing

> *"Email has an ability many channels don't: creating valuable, personal touches—at scale."*
>
> *– David Newman*

As organic social media becomes more difficult for company pages, then email marketing is once again being considered by many companies if they have a suitable opt-in GDPR compliant database.

A lot of businesses, especially smaller ones, are wary of email marketing due to GDPR and e-privacy laws. As long as you are aware of what you are and what you are not allowed to do, and you follow those rules then there is no reason that email marketing is not part of your marketing communications mix.

For detailed advice on those rules then visit the ICO website (https://ico.org.uk/for-organisations/guide-to-data-protection/guide-to-the-general-data-protection-regulation-gdpr/principles/).

If you are not sure if you should register with the ICO then there is a helpful self-assessment tool and lots of advice on their organisations section. (https://ico.org.uk/for-organisations/)

The ICO is not trying to catch anyone out, and if you have any questions then their helpline is very useful. If any doubt, then why not register anyway - £35 a year if paid by direct debit is a cheap way of giving your company credibility.

Now the legal bit is out of the way, if you have clients and prospects who have agreed to receive marketing communications from you, or you can state that there is a legitimate interest, then you should leverage email marketing. There are a variety of ways for email to benefit a company.

Lead nurturing

As the company generates enquiries through other marketing activities, then qualifying those enquiries into qualified leads can be done automatically through email waterfalls, where the actions taken by the recipient determine the next communications and when it is handed to sales.

This is achieved through lead scoring and by ensuring that BANTS (budget known, authority to make the decision, need clearly identified, timeframe is known, and they are sales ready).

Here is a simple example of how an email flow could be drawn out. The actions undertaken determine the next communication.

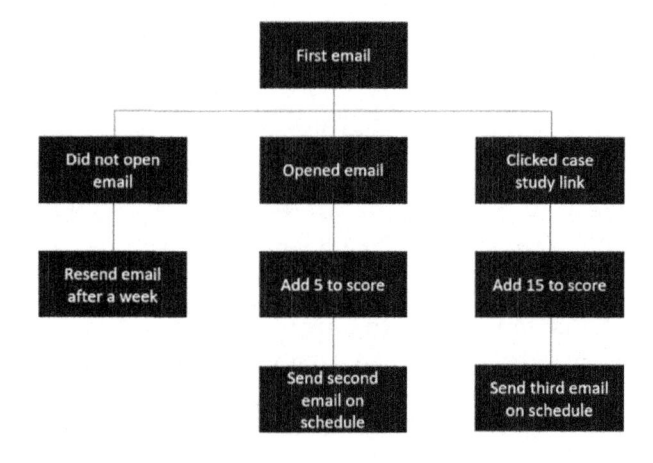

Figure 10: Example of Marketing Automation Flow

Let's talk through how the flows work. For example, it could be that the at a trade show there has been an enquiry. The first email may be the day that the enquiry was received, thanking them for coming by the stand and saying that you'll be in touch. Even in that short email, give an option of how they can speak to someone.

The next email may be an introduction to your company and the specific solution that they showed an interest in. If that email is not read, then it is resent a week later. If the email is opened but no action taken, then the next email is sent out in the series. However, if an action is taken – a link is clicked, a demo is booked – then that may mean that they jump forward in the cycle as each action has a score allocated to it.

Whereas it may sound complicated, it really isn't. It is simple if then logic – if prospect one didn't open the email, then send email2, if they did open the email but didn't click on any link then send email2 or email3 (depending on your content), if they clicked on a link then they fast forward to an email further down the sales funnel to secure that sale as early as possible.

You are listening to your prospects and giving them the next step that is applicable to them, automatically.

A lot of the email systems will allow you to put a score against an activity. When the prospect has acquired a certain score then they are passed to sales for follow up.

Keeping track of the responses is key. Earlier in my career there was someone who clicked a link from an email, they then downloaded 50 product specification sheets. That action from the email was quite a low score, but looking at what they had downloaded, each product specification sheet was gated at that time, meant that they became a hot lead, as each engagement was captured in the CRM. Sales were more than happy to engage as it converted really quite quickly.

There are tools such as Zoho Campaign, HubSpot or Mailchimp which all start with free of charge offerings. Review each and see which works the best for you. All of those have lots of help for you to set them up, or you could ask for external help.

Relationship marketing including newsletters

For previous clients, maintaining an ongoing relationship is important to ensure that for any future deals they automatically come back to you instead of looking at the whole of the market.

The trust that was won through the first deal together is remembered, even if the personnel have changed. The reinforcement of your brand is there.

Email can be used in two ways here (1) a regular newsletter or (2) specific invitations for events and activities.

A regular newsletter can be either a simple collation of PR pieces issued over the previous month or written specifically to a certain topic. In addition the newsletter can mention upcoming events and activities such as webinars, attendance at exhibitions or speaking slots at conferences or seminars. Even if the recipients do not attend, it reinforces in their minds that your company is a powerful, major force in the industry. Trust is built, thought leadership attained, together they lead to loyalty.

For the specific events as part of the pre-event marketing invitations can be sent using free tickets, if available, for a seminar / conference / exhibition that they would normally have paid to attend. You are showing that you value them as a client. That you are behaving as a partner not as a supplier. Again that fosters loyalty.

If the event is more around corporate hospitality, then email allows key personnel to be targeted, even if not your direct contact. For example, the budget holder instead of, or as well as, the technical advisor.

Specific campaigns

As the email database is built up, then specific email campaigns aimed at a certain vertical or geography can be devised. Whether it is a Did you know XYZ about your company with each email giving more insight into your full offerings, or a product launch, the announcement of a new affiliate partner and so on.

Email can be a cost-effective way of personalised but mass communication.

Tools needed

The database should be held in the single pot of truth that is your customer relationship management (CRM) software. Whether you are using the free of charge version of HubSpot or spending serious money on Salesforce, it doesn't matter. What does matter is that everyone uses it and updates it.

No Excel spreadsheets hiding on a laptop.

Having the data in one place allows more accurate segmentation. Avoids missing a core prospect out. Ensures that GDPR SAR (subject access requests) requests can be handled effectively.

For sending the emails, either your CRM offer emailing as an integral part (as HubSpot does) or it will link to one of many tools, such as MailChimp or

MailerLite, so that waterfall automations are set up and the unsubscribes are automatically captured.

Which the right tools for you are, depends on what you need from it in terms of ease of use, functionality and costs.

Direct mail

> *"Do you remember the 'You've got mail' jingle? And how excited people were when they received their first few emails? Now it's dreaded, and it's more exciting to check your mailbox than your email. Real mail also brings far less competition. And that's definitely good."*
>
> -Louis Camassa

You may ask why direct mail. Surely that has died a death, hasn't it?

Well yes, and no. The days of lots of junk mail, and it was junk as it wasn't well targeted, have fortunately gone. However targeted direct mail can work really well.

One of my clients targeted 50 key decision makers. It was a simple one-page letter, the name was handwritten in, the signature was done by hand on each letter, the envelope was handwritten. It stood out when it reached the target's desk as it looked personal, that someone had cared enough to take the time, and it is just so unusual. For those reasons, it was opened, and 30 people made enquiries. A printed name and address may have been deemed as junk mail and binned before being opened.

Costs were minimal, ROI was very high.

As part of a launch, another client used a Maltese cross mailshot.

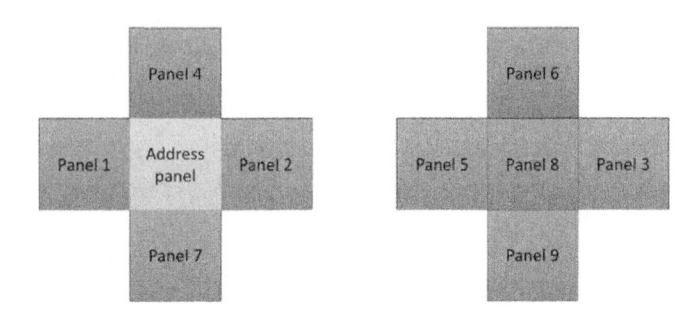

Figure 10: Maltese Cross with Panels Numbered as Seen When Opened

The panel numbers are the order in which they are read as it is unfolded by the recipient. You can tell quite a story. The folded cross is a square item, that can be posted easily – no envelope needed.

Another envelope free format can be a trifold (the printed item is folded twice so you are left with an envelope sized piece – 5 areas for messaging, one for the address and postage) with a sticker holding it shut.

There are plenty of printers who will help you with something a little different. Many of them also link up with mailing houses, so even though your list may not be long enough for discounts from Royal Mail, mailing houses can help you by merging your mailshot with another company's so that the postage rate is a fraction of a second-class stamp, let alone a first class one as they can use services such as Whistl.

Use direct mail to stand out. To not just be another email blocking up someone's inbox.

If you operate in a specific geography – maybe a takeaway or a new club, a hairdresser or a deli – then you can use Royal Mail services which are delivered to each household. In my area Farmfoods do that, even though the nearest one is about 8 miles away. Of course, results can be more hit and miss, but the delivery costs are so much lower.

At the time of writing according to the Royal Mail website, the cost for leafleting 8000 potential customers starts from £200. Of course the print costs are on top, but the delivery starts from 2.5p. Those prices are ex VAT.[20]

---

[20] https://www.royalmail.com/business-campaign/door-to-door/leaflet-distribution-pricing?cid=MR1119_D2DTEMP_SM_1001&cid=SM_RMB_0223&gad=1&gclid=EAIaIQobChMIy9S_0uaTgQMV9olQBh20lwBeEAAYAiAAEgKHwfD_BwE&gclsrc=aw.ds

Advertising

> *"Advertising is only evil when it advertises evil things."*
>
> *– David Ogilvy*

Display Online

To raise awareness then you may consider online display advertising in relevant publications, for example, a relevant trade publication's website, a membership body's website or even a national or regional newspaper's site.

There are various ways to reduce the costs, for example by choosing run of site – i.e. it turns up where they have space. This can lead to issues. One client placed an advert on a national newspaper site by run of site, it was shown next to an article about a violent murder and above a racy lingerie advert. Not exactly where they would ideally have been with their IT product.

The more specific the publication the less chance of that type of thing from occurring. The number of views may be lower, but the quality of the views being from your ideal customer profile will be so much higher.

However, you should be aware that more and more companies are installing advert blockers as standard to help in cyber security. That would mean that those display adverts would not be visible.

To avoid that, then maybe a sponsored post or advertorial in an email newsletter could be leveraged.

Offline

Printed publications are declining in their number and circulations, however, that does not mean that there is not a possibility of print advertising.

Instead of generic run of paper advertising, focus should be given to special editions or special features. Then a combination of display advertising and editorial could work very well together.

Do not be scared of looking on a publication's website for a "Media Pack" or "Editorial Calendar". A media pack should contain the editorial calendar as well as the advertising rates (those are the quoted rates, which no one pays, negotiate!). The editorial calendar will give dates of special editions, or topics that will have focus that week / month.

OOH (Outdoor)

OOH is just an industry term for advertising outside of the home.

As we will see below it is not just the huge billboards by the side of motorway going into a major city or the very large airport digital displays seen at Heathrow, but there are more subtle ways that are available to businesses of all sizes to raise awareness, even if it is sub-conscious at first.

Taxi advertising: **Within city centres, particularly London, the black cabs carry advertising on and inside them. Within the square mile in London the only advertising possible is on bus sides and taxis.**

There are a variety of options on the taxis: side panels (just the lower half of the doors), half-wrap (the bottom half of the taxi) or full wrap (the whole thing is covered). Some black cabs also have digital signage on the top.

During periods of turbulence or a stagnate economy the costs fall for this type of advertising, especially since the drop in commuter numbers following Covid and the rise of working from home.

There could also be a PR angle here as in a publicity stunt by running a competition over social media (X/Instagram/Facebook more so than LinkedIn) for people to snap the cab and post where they saw it.

Alternatively, book a wrapped cab for the day and take it to various sites where a professional photographer captures it, and those images are used in social media and PR pieces instead of relying on stock imagery. That way you stand out from the crowd.

Advertising inside the taxis can be good as you have a captive audience. However, the targeting is not as good as some other forms of advertising. If your offering is more generic, then it is something to be considered.

Bus advertising: On the outside of the buses there are adverts on the sides and on the backs. It is also possible to wrap a whole bus, but that tends to be the preserve of large B2C launches.

Inside buses there are also advertising spots that are restricted in size, but which people read as they are standing on the way to and from the office (far preferable to making eye contact with anyone else). These spots tend to be cheaper than the external spots, but the number of impressions will also be restricted.

For either of the bus options, targeting the bus routes that travel through the areas where your ideal customers are based is key. For example, if you have a software solution for legal companies, then the routes that go up and down Chancery Lane and The Strand (for the RCJ) in London would be key.

Tube advertising: There are various options here: in train, on platform, in station. This will not work for all companies, as TfL has guidelines about what they will allow and will not allow to be advertised re healthiness. They even went as far as removing an advert for a West End play as it had a wedding cake (high fat, high sugar) on it[21]. Check out their rules carefully.

In train: there are various adverts in every carriage. The Elizabeth Line, when used recently by the author, had approximately 20% of the advertising places empty, so a deal could be on the table there. If you are targeting financial institutions, then the Waterloo and City line would be a powerful location. However, the competition there is stiff, and instead of being one advert amongst a few visible to each person the whole content tends to be by one company on the whole train. That reduces the opportunities and exclusivity costs too.

On platform: Two options here – the large adverts across the tracks and the smaller adverts at the back of the platform. Again target the tube stations which are in the hot spot of your target audience. Some stations will be a lot more cost effective than others. Those further out of the city centre will be cheaper

---

[21]

https://www.google.com/url?sa=t&rct=j&q=&esrc=s&source=web&cd=&cad=rja&uact=8&ved=2ahUKEwje0rmk7JOBAxUOXEEAHcK0DMEQFnoECA0QAw&url=https%3A%2F%2Fwww.standard.co.uk%2Fnews%2Flondon%2Fsadiq-khan-wedding-cake-advert-tfl-tony-tina-ban-obesity-b1095815.html&usg=AOvVaw2g--d25B4jWIXUxsZOp6v5&opi=89978449

than those in the city centre, but then chances to be seen are also reduced.

In station: At Bank, the travelators to and from the Waterloo and City can be branded. Again, a big-ticket item. However, at the tube stations, there are other opportunities – by the escalators to and from the street level. Some stations have A2 posters, or even advertising on step risers as you leave the platform. As ever a careful analysis of footfall in the target demographic would be required to ensure coverage.

Radio

With the growth of commercial radio stations, radio advertising can be cost effective. A 30 second advert typically costs £2 per 1000 listeners at the time of writing, so careful targeting on stations and at time of day for the key demographics then it can be great at raising awareness. For example, if you are targeting IT Directors, talkSPORT during the morning rush hour may deliver far better results than the same advert on SmoothFM, as the gender split in IT is still a long way from 50/50.

Of course, you can also drill down to local commercial radio stations if you are operating in a certain geography instead of national wide.

With all advertising though remember whether it is online or offline, it needs to be integrated with a campaign to give the best results. Some of the other techniques we are about to go through may not need spend but can make your advertising more effective as the recognition of your brand is gaining ground.

PR

> *"Everything you do or say is public relations."*
>
> *– Unknown*

You don't necessarily need an expensive PR agency to deliver on press coverage. There are tools out there that can get you in front of top publications – it really is who dares wins sometimes.

In many cases, not having to brief a PR agency means that you can get the piece out quicker, especially if you have a very technical product. You are the expert in that case.

If you don't want to sit and type a piece up, then use dictate on your phone or laptop into Word and then upload to something like ChatGPT for it to be reworked or send out to someone to finalise it.

Press Releases

In these days of online publications, then need a lot more quality content than they did when purely paper based. They have to have new content each day. This gives you a lot more chance of getting your name out there.

Saying that, the press release has to be newsworthy (new product launch, acquisition, case study). If it is more an opinion piece, then either issue as a blog or get buy in from the publication / site before it is written to save you time and effort.

To be successful with press releases, then you need to build relationships with the editorial teams of your target publications. Even then not all publications will be equal in what they offer you in terms of reach and applicable readers.

One way to it do it is to split the media into tears.

Tier 1 media are those key publications / websites / programs / channels in your industry that have the reach to your Ideal Customer Profiles. Obtaining coverage in mass media may seem attractive, e.g., daily newspapers or magazine shows on the TV, but what impact does that have on those ideal audiences?

Interesting but not necessarily targeted media would be in Tier 2.

Use your time to build those personal relationships with the Tier 1. For the other publications, then use the newswire services that are available, although they do charge, they will get your PR piece in front of far more editors than doing it yourself.

Another option is to keep an eye on tools such as Cision's Speak to an Expert which was Help a Reporter Out previously. Three times a day emails are sent out listing subjects that journalists are writing about. Timescales can be quite short, but it can be worth it. The author responded to one journalist's request answering their questions in detail, they reformatted it, so it was as if she had been interviewed[22]. No-one else was quoted in the article. Great coverage. No fees paid.

Each time you issue a PR piece it should also be on your website under a News section and linked to from your social media too to generate traffic and

---

[22] https://www.iadvanceseniorcare.com/how-a-competitor-analysis-can-boost-your-marketing/

credibility. If you can achieve a back link from the third-party site, then that is fantastic.

Articles / Opinion Pieces

When the relationships with Tier 1 are formulated, then invitations to provide in depth articles or opinion pieces will follow more automatically. Such pieces position your company as a thought leader, a market influencer or driver, a serious player in your industry.

Articles and opinion pieces give confidence, credibility and gravitas that your ideal customers are looking for, plus possibly future funders and investors too.

The by-line of such pieces should be given to the company's spokespeople. Build up their brand and it will reflect positively on your company too, as it shows that you invest into a depth of knowledge and experts in the field. It is irrelevant who actually writes the content. It maybe that you have different spokespeople for different geographies or different areas of specialism when it comes to industry sectors.

Blogs

There are two ways to utilise blogs: having your own or being a guest contributor to another organisation's blog are important tools in the marketing mix.

Your own blog allows the depth of knowledge to be seen. It gives new content for the website, which in turn increases SEO and domain authority results. It encourages repeat visitors to the website. The blog should be issued so that it can be subscribed to – that increases the email list and allows analysis of the readership and if it is targeting the audiences as defined effectively.

Guest contributing gives valuable backlinks increasing the domain authority of the site, but also puts your company in front of new readers, who hopefully will then subscribe to your own blog and ultimately become clients.

Blog content can also be leveraged in a LinkedIn Newsletter or as social media posts. Recycling the messages across formats and platforms is frequently used for maximum impact.

It is unlikely someone reads the blog, every social post, the LinkedIn newsletter and so on AND remembers everything that they have read.

Case Studies (written and video)

Case studies are important for showing empathy. They demonstrate that you know what you are talking about, that you have delivered for other people and therefore reassure that your prospect will not be breaking new ground, but that it has been done before. Few companies want to be bleeding edge, cutting edge is far more preferable.

Video case studies are extremely powerful for use on social media. They take a little more arranging as the parties must be available in a similar timeframe, if not at the same time, and then there is editing to schedule. They can be used on your website, as part of presentations and social media. They may be picked up by third party websites as content too.

Ideally written case studies names will be used with quotations from key personnel, however, if this is not possible then it is possible to use, for example, "major bank" or "technology company". It does dilute the strength of the case study, but it can still be effective, even if just used internally to reinforce what is possible (sometimes called a Success Story). The author once had a case study that stated, "Global aircraft manufacturer with a HQ in Toulouse, France and factories in the UK and Germany." Anyone in the industry knew exactly who it was, but to avoid getting stuck in their legal team that was the work around that they suggested and signed off on.

The process for a case study should be that there is written agreement before the case study is drafted from the parties involved. Then a short interview takes place (in person or by sending email questions). The drafted case study is sent for review and approval by each party. The approver has to have the correct authorisation status for their organisation plus agree where the case study can be used (general, web site only, in presentations, in sales meetings, at conferences...)

A format that works well for a case study is SCRAP :

THE SCRAP FORMAT

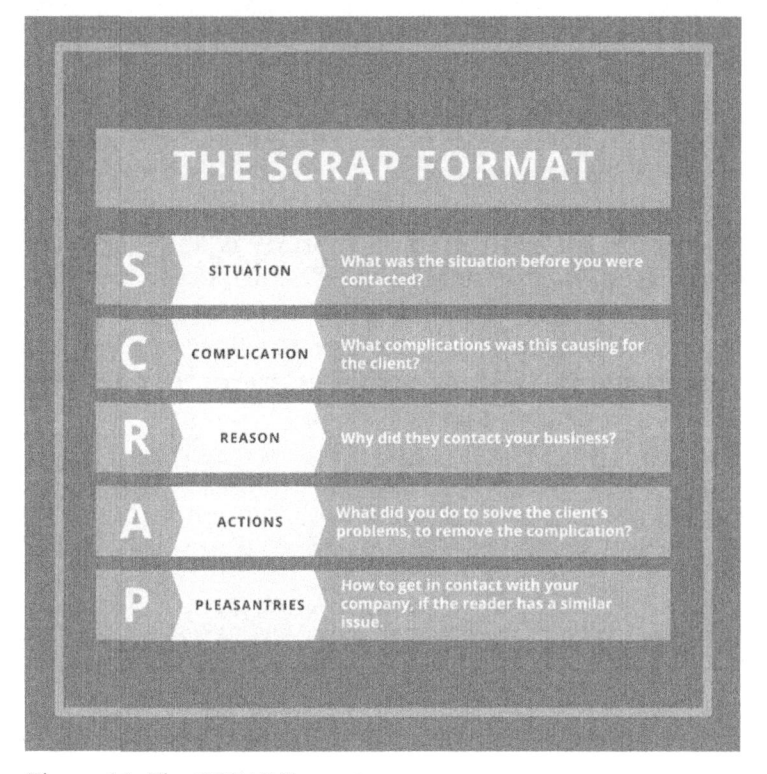

S	SITUATION	What was the situation before you were contacted?
C	COMPLICATION	What complications was this causing for the client?
R	REASON	Why did they contact your business?
A	ACTIONS	What did you do to solve the client's problems, to remove the complication?
P	PLEASANTRIES	How to get in contact with your company, if the reader has a similar issue.

Figure 11: The SCRAP Format

Case studies can be issued to the press, but they can also be part of an email campaign. For example, the author received an email mentioning that it contained a case study of the results of their services. The link in the email went to a landing page full of links to case studies covering different offerings. It was clear and quick to navigate. When the author clicked a link the case study itself was well structured and clear, even though no names were mentioned, there was enough detail to be credible.

It was a good campaign from the particular finance company, leveraging assets they already had and giving their various offerings credibility.

Testimonials (written and video)

Testimonials tend to be a short snippet or a quotation.

They are great for using on social media and as part of presentations. They give confidence to the reader / viewer.

Asking for testimonials should be an automatic thing. Don't be nervous, you'll be amazed how readily people will do them. Most people want to be helpful.

Video testimonials can be captured easily on a smartphone when you are in a meeting. Just remember to turn the camera landscape for a professional result. People are far more comfortable in front a camera than they used to be pre-pandemic thanks to all those video calls.

Of course, permission should be sought and gained before the testimonial is used.

White Papers

Longer and more in depth than articles or opinion pieces, white papers really emphasise the knowledge that is within your company.

They are not sales focused, as brochures may be, but instead are positioning documents. They increase the awareness and credibility of your company. As we discussed above, they can be gated on the website so that they are email list and lead generators. They can formulate the basis of presentations delivered at conferences or on webinars.

Podcasts

Quite a new tool in the marketing communications mix, podcasts still have novelty value, but can also get the message out to new audiences.

If you have enough content, or enough guest speakers, then consider having your own podcast. However, for many companies being featured on other podcasts is a better way to go.

A review of the best podcasts in the target audience sectors should be made to give a short list of podcasts to target.

Then if a guest on a podcast, social media content should refer to it by both your company and the podcast host. Backlinks also help with the SEO and Domain Authority growth.

E books

E books can be great from an SEO point of view, plus as a lead generator. They can be used to position your business as the expert in the field by issuing e books.

They would need to be updated on a regular basis to remain relevant.

There is also the possibility of listing e books on platforms such as Amazon. Not as a serious revenue generator but instead as a positioning piece. If the subject area is chosen carefully, it is possible to have the title Number 1 Bestseller, again building on gravity and credibility of the author and the company.

Events

> *"Good fortune is what happens when opportunity meets with planning."*
>
> *Thomas Edison*

During the pandemic there was a major impact on face-to-face events, and they have now started-up again. It may be worth while exploring sponsorship opportunities at applicable events – anecdotal evidence is that attendance levels at exhibitions and face to face events is now back to or surpassing pre-pandemic levels. It will be interesting to see if this continues as pre-pandemic attendance levels were dropping.

Events can range from a seminar or a roundtable discussion which is very targeted, to huge conferences and exhibitions which fill the Excel in London.

But think outside the box a little too. How about leveraging a pop-up? These can be as part of a collection of companies all in one particular venue, for example, the pop-up malls, Boxpark, in Croydon and Shoreditch, which uses shipping containers as bite sized venues and shops. These can help you to test a concept before investing in bricks and mortar premises.

Alternatively, you could grab a pop-up stand at a busy railway station if your target market is commuters, for example, London Liverpool Street or Manchester Piccadilly. Again, the pricing for these tends to fall during economically turbulent times, as there is a reduction in the number of companies wanting to use them, additionally as commuter numbers are still below pre-pandemic levels, so the number of people seeing the pop-up is reduced. Do not be afraid to ask and to negotiate if you feel the price is too high. You are in the stronger position not TfL or Network Rail!

Some shopping malls, if applicable to you, also have pop-up slots available. Again they are open to price negotiation.

Exhibitions

Walk through

Exhibiting itself is not always required. Sometimes it is about walking the exhibition to make new contacts, have conversations, generate business.

Before committing to exhibiting at any event it is recommended to walk the show the year before to really evaluate it instead of what is in the media pack for the event, especially if alongside a conference.

Exhibitor – online

Online exhibitions increased in popularity during Covid. Organisers were trying to find a way of keeping some income.

With online exhibitions though the pre-event marketing is so much more important. The attendees have to know enough about your company to actually look you up on the exhibitor list. There is no chance of accidental awareness as they walk past en route to another stand.

Engaging with stand visitors is also difficult. Very often the visitor has to start the conversation. There is no body language, it is difficult to see what they are particularly interested in. Sales staff get really annoyed, bored and fed up.

Exhibitor – in person

Turning up with a great stand is not the best thing to make a difference to results.

Exhibitions need a strong pre-event campaign so that stand is seen as a must visit stand. So that attendees put your business on their route map around the hall. Most visitors will know exactly who they want to talk to before they get there at B2B shows. You cannot rely on walk by traffic to hit the results.

When choosing a stand, location wins every time over size. Look at footfall direction, where strategic partners are, where competitors are. In the past, the author only had a budget for a 3m x 2m stand at Semicon West, San Francisco, but it was next to the entrance. Pre-event marketing about the innovative technology being announced had made it a destination stand, especially when the daily show newspaper carried PR on the company (we are talking pre-email newsletters and show apps here). A 3m x 2m stand with a queue of people wanting to talk about the new technology. Requests for quotation were through the roof.

It was the pre-event, at event and post-event marketing campaigns that made the real impact.

Exhibitions should be chosen carefully, especially if there is no speaking slot available.

Seminars and Workshops

These could be events that you participate at, but they are small conferences and are covered in the section below.

Here, we are discussing those face-to-face seminars and workshops that you take the lead on organising.

Have a clear subject. Have a clear target audience in mind. Do not feel that you have to be restricted to PowerPoint presentations. The best events have the most engagement so here are a couple of ideas that you can modify for your business.

The do what you've always wanted to do but didn't dare

We have all had the feeling that we want to see what happens, if we dare to do what should be possible. What would happen if it all went wrong? What would the impact on your business be?

If you have a brand-new smart phone in its new case that can apparently withstand being dropped on to concrete from a height of 35 metres with no damage to the case or the phone, would you test it?

Back in the late 90s, there was a new way of using Microsoft NT to "cluster" servers. The theory was that if one server failed for whatever reason then the other would take over. IT staff wanted to try this out for themselves but didn't dare in a live working environment. They wanted to see that it did indeed work.

At that time, the author was working in a company which set up a series of 1 on 1 meetings where we had various technologies set up in the "seminar" room we had hired, including clustered servers. We invited each attendee to pull the plug out of the wall for one of the two servers to see what would happen.

It was doing something that they wouldn't do themselves in a live environment, but it gave the confidence that they needed. Plus it gave the satisfaction of giving in to the little child within – something that is powerful in its own right.

You say such and such is unbreakable – prove it

Many of us will remember the Tonka Toy adverts from the 1970s and 1980s. If you don't then follow the hyperlink in the footnotes to YouTube[23] [24] they took demonstrating that their toys wouldn't break to extremes.

If you make a claim that your product will stand up to certain treatment or it's unbreakable, how about you prove it? A couple of years back, the brand has been forgotten now, the author was at the stand alongside this manufacturer at a large exhibition in Dubai. Every couple of minutes a sledgehammer was pulled back to horizontal on an arm, and then it was let go into the unbreakable screen that they were demonstrating. The bang was quite loud. Every two minutes from show opening to show closing for 4 days. The screen didn't break.

Another IT example from the early days of thin client computing, companies were nervous about the security of Citrix. The company the author worked for set up a workshop, we had a dozen IT directors and they each brought a true techie. You know the type of person – they hack through anything. We set up a Citrix network and told them to break into it. Two dozen people trying to break in at the same time, for over an hour. It didn't fail.

Those IT Directors were from FTSE100 companies. We were a small reseller (about 50 staff), and we

---

[23] https://www.youtube.com/watch?v=1oGjFGFA1OA

[24] https://www.youtube.com/watch?v=w565GRgnapA includes an elephant stepping on the toy and a car using the toy to support a flat tyre on a journey

picked up the orders because we dared to let them do what they wanted to do, we proved the claims.

If you are a food company, do blind taste testing.

If you are a joiner making bespoke conservatories, put in place a test that opens and shuts a door lock equivalent to 30 years' openings and closings, video it and play it on 10x or quicker speed to show the reality. That will make your 25-year warranty look very achievable.

Think of the things that attendees have wanted to do, will remember and will talk with other people about.

But I still want some PowerPoint

Yes, it has its place.

BUT

Do not put every word that you are about to say on the screen. Use images instead so that people listen to you instead of reading.

One of the best presentations the author ever saw was a guy who only had one slide. It was a photograph of deep space. The engagement levels in the auditorium were immense. You could have heard a pin drop, no sub-conversations between people in the audience, no one was reading emails or typing text messages. That speaker had everyone enthralled in his subject matter – and that is the point of a presentation.

Another excellent presentation the author saw that did use PowerPoint slides, caused a lot of laughter, confused faces with each new slide, and engagement, was one where every slide was just the abbreviation of what was to be covered. We all use Q&A as shorthand, but he had turned everything into acronyms, including his final slide which read

TTFN (ta-ta for now) in the days before LOL, OMG etc were in common parlance, it stood out – that presentation was back in 2003 and but is still remembered because it was so different.

What is the worst that can happen?

Many of us avoid presenting because we are scared of making a fool of ourselves, falling on the way on to the stage, losing complete track of what you are talking about next, the AV not working correctly.

But these things happen. It is what you do about it when it happens, if anyone even notices. That *"huge fall"* may have been a little trip; that silence that seemed to go on for ever whilst you remembered the next bit of the speech, was probably a fraction of a second.

If you do forget what you are talking about, take a deep breath and a sip of water. It gives time to recover.

If you drop all your notes on the floor – make a joke about it. Don't have the audience laugh at you, know that they are laughing with you.

At a concert the author attended the jazz singer totally lost the words to the song part way through. She had a conversation in melody and rhythm with the pianist until her brain "rebooted" as she put it.

Were the audience annoyed? Did they demand a refund? No! They loved it. Their idol was human!

Conferences

Being asked to deliver a keynote or breakout is excellent for coverage.

Keynotes being to the whole attendee audience, can get the message in front of new prospects. Being a keynote gives the acknowledgement of the power of the organisation and the knowledge within the organisation. It is the organisers promoting trust and belief in and on behalf of your company.

Breakout sessions can really help to separate the wheat from the chaff of the main auditorium. If the session is selected, then there is a genuine interest from the participants.

Conferences should be reviewed, synopses delivered according to deadline (if needed) and relationships with organisers built.

Sometimes instead of a dedicated slot it will be an interview on stage, or a panel discussion. Preparation for all formats is key. Never forget Proper Planning and Preparation Prevent Pathetically Poor Performance when going up on stage – it will help to calm nerves if you suffer from them.

Evaluating which conference or exhibition to pay to play at is a combination of things: numbers of new (i.e., not current clients) target audience attending, estimated number of enquiries, estimated size of deal at what profit level, conversion rates from that type of activity and the costs involved. Not just the participation fee but also the travel and entertainment expenses, any logistic and / or production costs if there is a stand as well, pre-event and post-event marketing as well as lost opportunity costs of not being in the office that day for those attending.

Write yourself a business case with clear objectives for every event that you do and monitor your responses.

Webinars

Webinars, and their cousins Facebook and LinkedIn Lives, are very powerful tools. The costs in hosting them are a lot less than a face-to-face event, plus the geographical spread of attendees can be far wider.

Keep them short 20 – 30 minutes of content, absolute maximum of 45 minutes, then allow 15 – 30 minutes of Q&A time.

Keep the subject targeted. One that your customers are already asking you about – if they are then it is probably going through the heads of your prospects too. Give a solution so that you are seen as a trusted adviser and watch the enquiries come in.

Each webinar should be recorded, ensure everyone knows that it is before they log on. You can then upload it to your website, possibly behind a data capture form to see who is looking at your content. If they give permission for marketing messages, then that will help to build your database.

More people can schedule an online session into their day, than the additional time commitment of travelling to a face-to-face event. A win-win situation, more attendees, less cost.

In addition, the pre-event marketing raises the brand awareness, they provide strong content that can be converted to white papers and vice versa, snippets can be used for video posts on social media, recordings can be viewed later on your website.

If you can build a series, then that can build credibility and awareness in the marketplace. Announcing the series dates ahead of time, allows you to be accountable, but also allows people to plan their time effectively and ensure that you are in before other events, meetings and activities swallow that time up.

Capturing registrations can help to build out the email list, as well as being lead generators in their own right.

If you are a MS365 user, then MS-Teams has a webinar option, so no additional software is needed. Currently with M365 Business Standard licenses the maximum number of attendees per webinar is 300 – more than enough for most SME events.

Webinars can also be delivered in conjunction with industry publications. These joint webinars help with establishing you as a thought leader, as a company pushing your industry forwards. They also get you out in front of people who don't already know you.

Market Intelligence / Surveys

> *"The essence of strategy is choosing what not to do."*
>
> *- Michael Porter*

Being a company that completes regular surveys of the state of your industry is a powerful tool for PR coverage, for webinar content, for white paper content. In addition, it lifts the company above others in the industry, as you are clearly invested in the market for the long term.

Think about surveys which regularly hit the headlines such as the S&P Global/ CIPS (Chartered Institute of Procurement and Supply) Purchasing Managers' Index[25], which indicates how positive the economy is feeling at the moment. CIPS have been holding this survey for many years.

EY disclosed results of a survey conducted in late 2020 and again in 2022 around the Covid-19 impact. They interviewed just 200 senior-level (their term) supply chain executives.

The results were referred to in various publications and on platforms such as LinkedIn by third parties – i.e. EY issued the report and others marketed it for them.

EY themselves are not a supply chain specialist, but they took the opportunity.

How do you get the number of people to give decent results? One way is to use social media to

---

[25] https://www.cips.org/intelligence-hub/pmi

recruit responses to a quarterly online survey to allow the quantity needed.

Ask the same questions each time and that will allow you to capture statistics and trends. There are plenty of tools out there that will help you with online surveys from MS-Forms (part of MS365) and GoogleForms to SurveyMonkey (free if less than 10 questions and 10 respondents)[26] to QuestionPro (free account with 30 different question types)[27].

If in-depth data is needed, then consider detailed telephone surveys or a focus group, whether face to face or online, with a smaller audience. They are more costly to implement, so start with online surveys as a first step.

---

[26] https://www.surveymonkey.com/pricing/individual/details/?ut_source=pricing-teams-details

[27] https://www.questionpro.com/pricing/

Relationship Marketing

> *"Relationships are like muscle tissue. The more they're engaged, the stronger they become."*
>
> *- Ted Rubin*

The costs associated with finding new clients, resellers and affiliates are often estimated to be 8-10 times higher than maximising the relationships and share of wallet with current clients by utilising cross-selling and upselling, after all you are already trusted.

Never overlook your current clients. They are providing the funds today for the marketing for you to grow tomorrow.

That makes relationship marketing very important to hit the growth targets that you have, especially with the uncertain geopolitical and economic climate at the moment. By building the relationships then the opportunity for repeat business, cross and up selling increases.

It needn't cost a lot. It just has to be relevant. It has to have value for them. Whether that is a newsletter with tips and tricks to get the best out of your product or service. Whether it is a report on how the market is, which points out that it is not all doom and gloom out there. Whether it is an email which allows them to see that you've not forgotten about them and that they are valued.

Almost 30 years ago, very early in the author's career, a newsletter was pulled together of the PR articles that had been issued in the last 3 months for current customers. It was printed on the laser printer (no email back then). Folded by hand and put into envelopes.

It was a new idea the author had floated, and as budgets were small, it was tried.

Now in that particular industrial niche there were two groups of customers. Those who used Product A and those who swore blind for Product B. The company produced both. Usually there were no crossovers. Or that was the recognised thinking at the time. So the sales guy never mentioned the other product set on his visits.

BUT, with that newsletter a current client phoned the sales guy and said that they were not aware of the company providing Product B. Yes, they used a certain amount of Product A per year, but they used 10 times the amount of Product B. They asked for a quotation. They consolidated the purchasing to one company – the one that provided both.

One newsletter that had a massive ROI in terms of percentage.

Never be afraid of telling your customers about everything that you offer. Don't project your beliefs onto them. You could be losing out on major sales.

Don't necessarily send a catalogue of absolutely everything, but in the regular communications that you do send out, mention other products or services that you could offer. Even if it is not for them, they may recommend you to someone else.

If you are in Business to Business, it is important that your sales team fosters a diamond account basis rather than a bow-tie model. That way it is not so catastrophic if one person either at your company or the target company leaves or is on elongated sick leave for example. The relationships between the two businesses are far stronger than that.

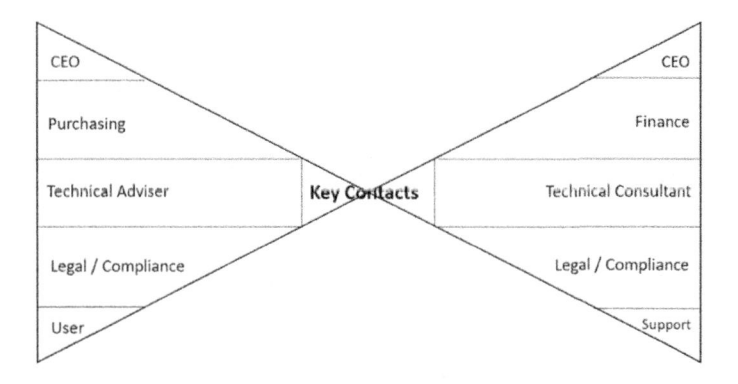

Figure 12: Bow-tie structure, with one example of functions, the left is the customer, the right is your company.

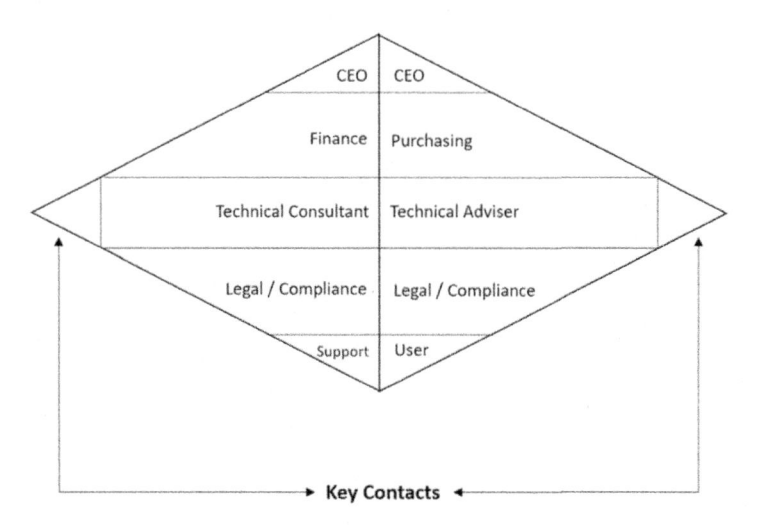

Figure 13: Diamond Structure, with same sample functions as above.

You are building a relationship with the individuals and the company.

Thrive, Not Just Survive

Word of Mouth Marketing and Referrals

"A customer talking about their experience with you is worth ten times that which you write or say about yourself."

- David J. Greer

Your customers should be your biggest advocates. They could be a powerful sales engine for you by recommending you to others.

Many companies try to have influencers of various types speak about their offerings, forgetting that their customers can be the biggest influencers of all.

You can't control the word-of-mouth marketing. You can't insist that it is done. But you can deliver such a great customer experience and service that they want to tell others about you. They want you to succeed. They want others to have the same product or service that they have.

You can help it along by offering a referral fee or reward. Now for some regulated industries this can be a keyway of getting new clients. For others, it is part of the overall marketing mix.

Before you put a scheme into place. You need to consider the impact on your profitability. If you are running on slim net profit margins of 10%-15%, don't offer a referral fee of 10% of the invoice, unless you know that there is repeat business, and you only pay out on the first invoice.

You need to consider who you want to reward. Is it companies who don't buy from you but can recommend you to your clients. For example, in the IT world, one company may say that the solution to the client's issue is XYZ, which is not provided by them but is complementary to them. The client then asks, "where do I get that?" and the IT company can recommend an alternative IT provider to close the gap. The original IT company has the trust of the client, so their recommendation is followed, and they earn a little bit more from the deal.

Where this can be very powerful, is if another company is always in the project earlier than your company would be because of the order of things. For example, if you are a groundworker, then you may pay a referral fee to an architect but get a referral fee from a builder who takes the project from ground up once you're finished. If you are a body work garage, you may pay a referral fee to an insurance company to have a steady stream of work. You may give a discount against your subscription box for customers who give their family and friends a code and they become customers.

Referral fees differ from loyalty schemes as it is about growing the network and your client base.

Loyalty Schemes

> *"It is not your customer's job to remember you, it is your obligation and responsibility to make sure they don't have the chance to forget you."*
>
> *- Patricia Fripp*

You will know about American Express points or cashback for everything that you spend. Or Nectar that you collect from various companies including eBay, Sainsburys, Esso and Argos. The miles that a frequent flyer can earn. The stamp cards or apps that you can use in coffee chains.

The loyalty scheme ensures that you return to that provider time and again as you are being rewarded.

In a business-to-business context it is more likely that you will be able to negotiate a discount on purchases as opposed to rack rates, just because you buy again. Companies who supply printer toner cartridges often do this as they are in a commoditised market.

How can you use loyalty schemes?

Evaluate the impact on profitability by offering the free coffee on the Xth visit, a free bottle of salon shampoo when so much spent, a free external car wash after three valets or whatever you decide.

Try and make it easy for your customer. Small cardboard cards that you cross or stamp can be produced cheaply and can be handed out easily at the till. Then they can be slipped into the credit card slots for the next visit.

If you have an app already, then explore how you can add loyalty on to there.

If you are an e-commerce site, then monitor the returning customer purchases and give a "free gift" after so many orders or email them a discount code to say thanks for 3 orders so far this year.

M&S are clever with their Sparks scheme. Each purchase earns money for a charity chosen by the customer. Each purchase has the chance to be that week's branch winner for their shopping for free. There are no points or guaranteed rewards for the customer, but there is that chance that the weekly shop or the new boots will be free, and the warm fuzzy feeling of supporting a charity without having to spend anything themselves.

There are a lot of ways of building a loyalty scheme into your marketing mix, no matter how big or small you are. It has to have enough value to be attractive to the customer and protect your profitability.

Sales Promotions

"Promotional pricing is a powerful tool, but if overused or implemented poorly, it can lead to a price orientation among customers, thereby diminishing the perceived value of your brand. Thus, it's critical to have clear objectives when implementing promotional pricing"

- Moira McCormick

Do not fall into the DFS trap, and always have a sales promotion running. DFS are now spending a lot of money trying to get away from that reputation that they have had for decades.

Do not run sales promotions to "channel stuff" if you are a manufacturer, it only harms your ongoing sales and costs you margin.

Only get involved in "Black Friday" and "Cyber Monday" if it makes sense for you to do so, not because everyone else is.

Sales promotions should have clear targets. A clear purpose. And be used sparingly. Then they can be very effective at increasing footfall or site visits and placed orders.

You can give a discount, bundle slower moving products up with faster moving products, run a 3 for 2 – there are so many possibilities.

One possibility that is overlooked by a lot of companies is the insurance backed competition or promotion. Did you ever wonder how McDonald's could give away a house, cars, holidays and so on with their Monopoly? Well, they, like many companies, use insurance backed competitions. The cost of the activity is a fraction of the cost of the prizes, as the chances of them being won are low.

But they don't need to be huge competitions like that. They can be much smaller. For example, you may decide that in your kebab shop, every customer that comes in and buys a kebab, has one chance to enter a digital code to open a safe, or a enter a code on to a website quoting the time and date on their receipt.

In that safe could be a cheque for £100,000, the keys to a Tesla Model 3, a 5* luxury all-inclusive holiday for 15 nights for a family of 4. It is the prize that encourages people to come in, buy a kebab and try and win the prize.

The insurance company then evaluates their risk. How long will the safe be there for? How many customers would be served typically without the promotion? What kind of increase would be expected due to the competition? How many digits are in the code that have to be entered – 6 there would be a 1 in 999,999 chance of it being entered correctly, 5 and the odds drop to 1 in 99,999 so the insurance premium would increase.

There are specialist insurance companies for this, but the costs can be a lot lower than you'd think for the noise that you can make with your social media and other activities that you are doing anyway! You may need a couple of extra posters for the shop window, or a specific banner on your website, but all very affordable.

Why not think outside the box and do something different?

If you are business to business, then insurance backed competitions can still work. It's all about the competition and how it is marketed.

Internal Marketing

> *"Internal marketing is probably much more important than external marketing. That's even more true today than it's ever been."*
>
> *- Tom Stewart*

It is easy to forget to keep staff up to date and informed. That can lead to the rumour mill taking hold. Now we all know that the rumour mill is not a reliable source of information, during turbulent times, with the headlines of job layoffs and big names going under (for example Wilko), then if a doubt is raised about your company, it is more likely to be believed.

To prevent a rumour becoming a self-fulfilling prophecy, it is key to be transparent, to encourage values to be shared, a common culture to be installed. In these days of remote and hybrid working internal marketing is absolutely essential.

Be honest with your employees.

If the company is cash-rich, then tell them that their salaries are safe for however many months without selling anything. They won't stop working, they will be relieved, and morale will improve. High morale tends to lead to higher productivity.

Be honest.

If the company is going to need to reduce wage bill, then talk it through. Not as part of a pre-redundancy consultation, but as people. During the financial crisis, some employees at a small engineering company decided to all take a 20% pay-cut instead of 20% of the workforce being laid off. The company kept valuable skills and came out of the recession quicker and salaries were put back up again.

Another company put a bonus in place depending on profitability. It made everyone aware of every penny that was spent, and they asked themselves if it was needed. Their electricity bill reduced as lights were switched off. The thermostat was turned down a degree in the winter and up a degree in the summer to reduce heating and air conditioning.

Ask for ideas.

Those on your front line will have ideas that they have kept to themselves. They may well be ideas on how to increase sales or reduce costs.

Building relationships with staff encourages loyalty, improves morale and motivation. Holding frank all company meetings about sales and profit performance proves transparency and increases accountability and responsibility to every employee. They feel more invested in the company's success.

It does not have to be complex, and it can be owned by either HR or marketing, but it should be done. Whether it is a regular newsletter, an intranet, or a fun charity activity, it all counts.

Campaigns can also be useful. In the past the author has run the below campaigns for specific purposes:

- Mind the Gap: yes, it was a variation to the tube map. Each tube line was a function or department. Each station something that they were responsible for so that the overall strategy was achieved, and the interchange stations, areas where they were dependent on or working with another department. It was printed up and put on the wall in each office location across EMEA and helped with prioritisation. Cost: design was done in-house printed on colour laser printer to A3.

- Success Breeds Success: during the financial crisis it was important to celebrate wins, no matter how small. The sales guys informed of their closed deals each week. There was a moving chart of who had closed what value. It wasn't just a sales competition; it was about recognition of the hard work being put in. Also seeing others be successful, meant that they realised that even though the headlines were doom and gloom business was still being done. It encouraged and empowered the team. Cost: a crate of wine for the winner after three months.

- Go to Green: A campaign that involved all departments and personnel. A campaign that highlighted that everyone in the company had a role to play in the company's success. That everyone could impact the company by hitting their KPIs and keeping an eye on costs and therefore help to push the company out of the red to amber and then to green on the KPIs. People realised that whatever they were responsible for they could make a difference – from the receptionist remembering to "lock" the franking machine at night (there had been a temp who franked £200 worth of envelopes!), to inside sales suggesting other items that were normally ordered at the same time, to the last person out of the office turning out the lights and ensuring monitors were off. Cost: nothing but communication.

- The water fight event: Charity events which got everyone involved. The water fight event was in response to severe floods in Pakistan and meant a lot to our rep out there. People paid to throw wet sponges at the Pricing Manager & Operations

Manager. In addition, staff brought in homemade cupcakes and samosas and sold them. The simplest idea was having everyone empty coppers out of their pockets – the chain on the floor went through the office and amounted to over £40. The water fight event raised over £1000 with about 60 employees.

- The custard pie event was for cancer research. Again, people bid for the right to put the custard pie in other people's faces. Food was again sold, and the coppers done. Again, over £1000 raised. Both events showed that senior management had a sense of fun too. Laughter brought the whole company closer together. Costs: Nothing, just a little time to send the emails and to make the custard pies.

Integrating the tools together for better results

> *"Integrated marketing communications is a way of looking at the whole marketing process from the view point of the customer."*
>
> *- Philip Kotler*

Each of the tools above can have results when used independently BUT for the best results use various of the tools in combination.

For example, you are about to launch a new product to the market. Here's how you may combine the aspects together.

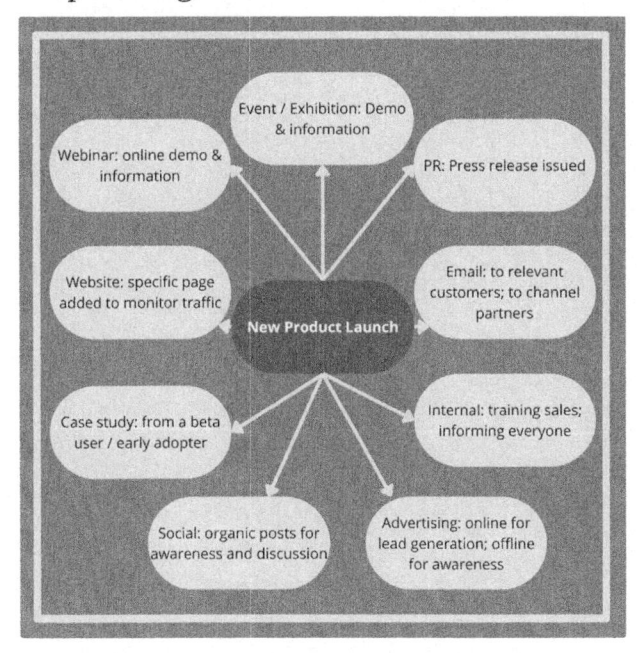

Figure 14: Combining the marketing mix together

This leads to a synergy effect. Someone sees the PR piece, then a little later the LinkedIn post, so they visit the web page, a webinar catches their interest which was advertised in an email, the webinar mentions a case study so that they are not bleeding edge but cutting edge – the prospect invites in your salesperson who has all the training needed on the benefits of the solution and not just the features.

Each tool reinforces the other marketing tools. They make your campaigns stronger and increase the ROI, without having to increase the marketing budget. Indeed the synergy in the paragraph above is achieved with little or no extra spend, just your time. You are maximising the value from each asset (case study, web page, email) with the reuse and integration.

Partnering for Success

> *"Alone we can do so little; together we can do so much."*
>
> — *Helen Keller*

What is a strategic alliance and why are they important?

A strategic alliance is a loose agreement between two companies. It is not a joint venture, but instead they are in complementary fields and help to promote each other or do joint go to market activities as a total solution.

They are frequently used in the IT sector. So companies such as Cisco and Panduit (a structured cabling manufacturer), as an example, will work together. In this case, Panduit is the smaller company and Cisco a household name BUT it is Panduit which is earlier into the deals for datacentres than Cisco due to the cabinets and cabling needed. Panduit introduce Cisco into the deals as a joint solution provider not as a reseller or an affiliate.

Panduit attend Cisco events, such as Cisco Live, to have access to their audience, and Cisco participate in Panduit events such as roadshows or their channel conference. In addition, Cisco and Panduit launched a training scheme at Wandsworth Prison, where the participants were guaranteed a job on release if they passed.

The two partners in a strategic alliance have different aims and objectives, but they do share some common ground and it is on that that they collaborate, increasing brand awareness and sharing marketing costs, being an advocate for each other.

Resellers & Distributors

In the place section above we discussed the various types of channel partner, so that content will not be repeated here.

Resellers allow you to have a virtual sales team at your disposal. If you have 100 resellers and they have one person working on selling your offering for ½ a day a week, that is like having an additional 10 salespeople. The author has worked with companies that have had tens of thousands of resellers, so just see how that grows your sales team with no risk to yourself, but with lower margins, as they have to be able to make money too.

Analyse which resellers are working the best for you. Focus on supporting them. That may not be the resellers that have the largest sales revenues, but the ones who proactively work with you to uncover new clients and contracts.

It used to be that 80% of your sales would come from your top 20% of resellers. However, in the days of Amazon that is not necessarily the case, as firms like Amazon hoovers up purchases but do nothing to grow the overall market or promote your solution over your competitors.

So when calculating your 20% of top resellers you may want to put to one side some of the large ecommerce companies.

If you go through a distribution channel to the resellers / retailers, then you need to understand exactly who they are selling to, how much and how regularly. You can obtain this information by asking them for POS (point of sale) information. This would give you a list of companies that they have sold your offerings to, how much and how frequently.

Why is that important?

The author worked with a company where she asked the MD how many resellers they had across EMEA. He was confident when he said 8,000. However, when we conducted POS analysis it was 16,000 that bought at least once a year and over 30,000 that bought every 2 years. So instead of 800 virtual salespeople, his company had 3,000, 2,400 of whom they knew nothing about!

The company was ignoring the majority of their channel. There was no relationship at all. No training (a loss of revenue stream there), no joint marketing activities, no support being given, no tools to help them sell more.

A lot of work was done to build those relationships. To identify who were the key influencers in each geography and vertical sector.

When identifying the correct channel partners to work with there are various areas that need to be looked at:

1. The total size of the market
2. Which resellers / distributors have the largest percentage of the market by geography (whether region or country)
3. Which resellers / distributors have the largest percentage of the market by vertical sector
4. Which partners your competitors use
5. Which partners complementary companies use
6. How the resellers and distributors fit together – you need to make it easy for resellers by working with a distributor that they already have an account and relationship with.

It takes time to build the correct coverage map, but it is worthwhile and makes a huge difference to your potential sales.

Section III: Marketing Measurement and Adaptation

> *"Without the right marketing metrics, you are shooting in the dark. The only way to know if things are working for you or not is those metrics."*
>
> — Ian Brodie

Key Marketing Metrics to Monitor: Identifying and tracking essential performance indicators.

"Not everything that can be counted counts, and not everything that counts can be counted."

- Albert Einstein

Of course you want to know that the marketing that you are doing is making a positive difference. You may see an uptick in sales, but how can you be certain that it is directly related to the activities that you are doing?

You need to measure the actions that you are taking, but you don't want to be spending all day everyday measuring. Some measurements are valuable, some are not.

Earlier, SMART objectives were defined. These should be done for your year overall but also for each campaign.

In table 3 you will see some of the things that you should measure, and some of the things that you really shouldn't waste your time in measuring.

Don't worry about all those lovely jargon abbreviations as we are going to go through those now.

Firstly, what is the difference between a hard and a soft measurement? A hard measurement tends to impact the bottom line either immediately or in the future after further nurturing. Soft measurements are the nice to haves, they are

What	Do Measure	Don't Measure
Campaign	**Hard measures:** ROI; Number of leads; Number of opportunities; Value of pipeline; Value of sales; CPA; LTV **Soft measures**: Number of testimonials; Number of case studies; Amount of PR coverage (as an equivalent advertising cost is also a possibility); Increase in opt-in database	Anything that appears below in this column
Social Media	Engagement: likes, comments, shares, mentions, clicks to website, video completion rate; Social selling: Clicks that buy from landing page	Number of followers – vanity!
Advertising - online inc SEM	CPC (Click); CPC (Conversion); CPA; LTV; CPM; ROAS; CTR;	
Website	Unique Visitors; Dwell time; Bounce rate; Source; Demographics (if important to you); Downloads; Purchases; Abandoned Carts; Top Pages; Top Exit Pages	Anything that doesn't give you relevant and valuable information to you. GA can be a rabbit hole of interesting but not impactful
Events	Attendance vs Booked vs Target; Number of leads; Number of opportunities; Pipeline value; Sales value; ROI; PR interviews held	If an exhibition total number of attendees - just measure those relevant to you
Referrals	Number and value of referrals; Cost of those; CPA	
PR	Number of articles, references, quotations in relevant publications; Equivalent cost compared to advertising	References on click-bait sites
Conversion Rates	From Enquiry to Qualified Lead From SQL to Opportunity From Opportunity to Sales	

Table 3: What to measure and what not to measure

woollier and are not directly linked to your bottom line. A combination of both will be a well-rounded campaign.

Now for the explanations:

ROI – return on investment – how much extra revenue have you achieved because of the marketing spend. Typically expressed as a percentage and it should always be positive. (If it is negative then have a look as to why that is so).

$$\frac{\text{Additional Revenue Achieved} - \text{Cost of Activity}}{\text{Cost of Activity}} \times 100$$

Number of leads – these are sales qualified leads, not just general enquiries. Don't see those people who just dropped their card into the goldfish bowl at the exhibition for a chance to win an iPad as leads – they are not. There has to be a relevance to your company and to the prospect.

Number of opportunities – the number of leads where you have quoted or given an idea of the costings to.

Value of pipeline – the total quoted amount of all the opportunities that have not yet closed.

Value of sales – the total amount of the sales as a result of the campaign.

CPA – cost per acquisition. So if you have spent £10,000 and have secured 100 new clients then your CPA would be £100. Different industries have drastically different acceptable CPAs.

LTV – lifetime value. It is all well and good having a new client, but what you really want is a client who keeps coming back time and again. If, for example, you were a beauty salon and you ran a campaign to have new clients, then you don't want them to come just once, but you want them to come back several times a year for their nails, a facial etc and you want them to remain loyal for several years. The total amount that they spend with you is their lifetime value.

CPC (Click) – confusingly CPC has two definitions, well that is the problem with TLA (three letter abbreviations), so be clear which one you are talking about. Cost per click is the amount you are paying each time someone clicks through on your advert (SEM or display). You want this figure to be as low as possible whilst still providing the required number of leads.

CPC (conversion) – very similar to CPA above. It is the cost per conversion, i.e. someone who buys from you or completes the action that you want them to complete.

CPM – cost per thousand. This is used for charging for display adverts per thousand impressions of your advert. An impression is it being shown once on a screen, no action has to take place, it was just there on the screen while the prospect was on that screen.

ROAS – return on advertising spend, basically the ROI as a result of just the advertising. That can be difficult to measure if you have a fully integrated campaign using various marcoms tools not just advertising.

CTR – click through rate is the number of people that click on your advert as a percentage of those who saw (the number of impressions) the advert.

Dwell time – the length of time that someone actively stays on your site. If they are going from page to page and spending time, then they are interested in your offerings.

Bounce rate – this is one that has disappeared from GA4 (Google Analytics 4). It is the number of people who land on a page and immediately leave again. The reason it is dropped from GA4 is that if someone goes to a landing page and buys immediately then leaves (all very possible) then they would be classed as a bounce when actually they are a conversion.

Source – where the web visitor came from. Was it social media, if so which one, if display advertising which site. It all helps you define where future spend is going to be placed.

Abandoned carts – we've all done it. Put something in the cart or basket on an online shop and then we've closed the site before completing the order. You want to know the value of those sales. You also want to see if there is a common drop off reason, maybe the delivery costs became apparent, maybe your system wouldn't accept a top level domain such as .marketing or .services as it didn't end in .com or .uk (The author has recently had this experience with Nationwide Building Society and surprisingly Fortnum & Mason while attempting to buy a gift), maybe the delivery time was too long. Some of these you would have to suppose, but if you can find a solution then it could reduce your abandoned carts and increase your sales.

Top pages – the most frequently visited pages. Are they as you would expect? Anything unusual that you could leverage?

Top exit pages – the page from which the visitor most frequently leaves. If that is a thank you for your order page, then nothing to worry about, but if it is an abandoned cart then you have an issue.

Attendance vs booked vs target – when you are setting up your seminar you should have an ideal number of attendees in mind. How does that compare to the number of people who booked a seat? Did you sell out? Were you oversubscribed? (can you put a duplicate event on a different date if the room capacity is not there?) Of those who booked, what were the attendance levels like? It is very rare to have 100% of bookings attend especially if it is a free of charge event.

PR interviews held – whether journalists, bloggers or influencers in your niche, how many interviews have you arranged?

Costs of referrals – in the B2B sector many companies offer a finder's fee for a referral that converts. That can be a fixed amount; a percentage of the first month's invoice or an ongoing percentage of all invoices for the lifetime of the customer. If you are offering a referral fee, then build it into your costings and ensure that you are not eroding your net margin too much.

Conversion rates – so that you can tell ahead of time if an activity is going to be successful for you, you should know your conversion rates. The first one is rate of conversion from enquiry to qualified lead. The second is from sales qualified lead to opportunity, the final one from opportunity to sale. Many people think that marketing is all about putting things into the top of the sales funnel as enquiries, but if you can improve your funnel efficiency then the results can be huge. Take a look at the below diagram to see just how big. Now the figures on the right are ones from a company the author worked at; the figures on the left well the 0.1% conversion from opportunity to customer was what one company had when they gave me their figures. Spending money on marketing tools to improve conversion rates is a far better investment than just keeping tipping in at the top.

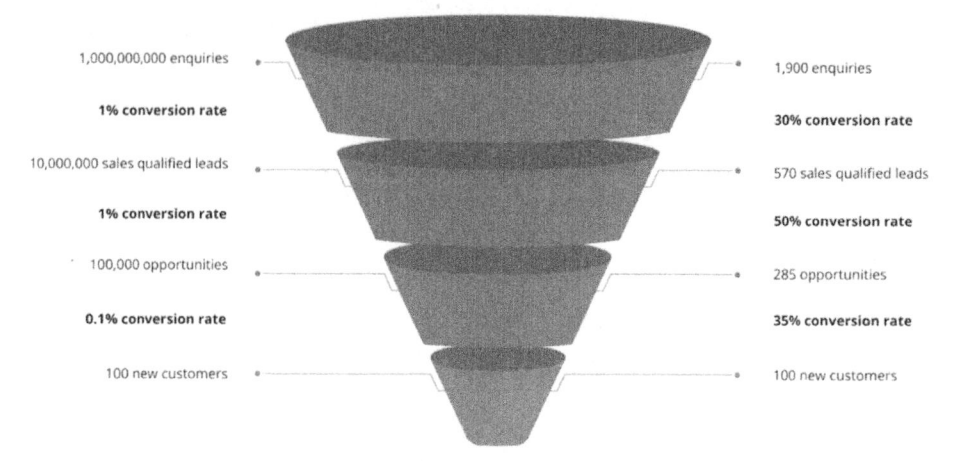

```
1,000,000,000 enquiries                              1,900 enquiries

    1% conversion rate                               30% conversion rate

10,000,000 sales qualified leads                     570 sales qualified leads

    1% conversion rate                               50% conversion rate

    100,000 opportunities                            285 opportunities

    0.1% conversion rate                             35% conversion rate

    100 new customers                                100 new customers
```

Figure 15: Conversion rate implications

Hopefully, it is now clear why you should measure and an indication of the types of things to measure.

After a major campaign or event, then have a debrief session. Leave job titles at the door. Concentrate on what could have been done better, constructive comments only and allow everyone to speak.

No such thing as a bad idea for improvement, and everyone's opinion is equal.

The author witnessed a timid marketing assistant grow in confidence as she found the courage, with encouragement, to tell the MD that he had made her job more difficult at a conference because he had ignored the 3-minute, 1-minute and cut now hand signals. He overran, quite considerably. That meant that the agenda had to be reshuffled. The time for networking was shortened. The refreshments had to be retimed with the venue. The MD agreed that he had allowed his ego to get the better of him, and that he would not allow that to happen again. He had not considered the impact his overrun would make to other people, or the overall success of the event by curtailing the networking opportunities by shortening breaks.

The debriefs only need to be an hour, but capture the improvements, the learnings for next time and move forwards. After all constant improvement is a repetitive cycle.

PLAN → BRIEF

CONSTANT IMPROVEMENT

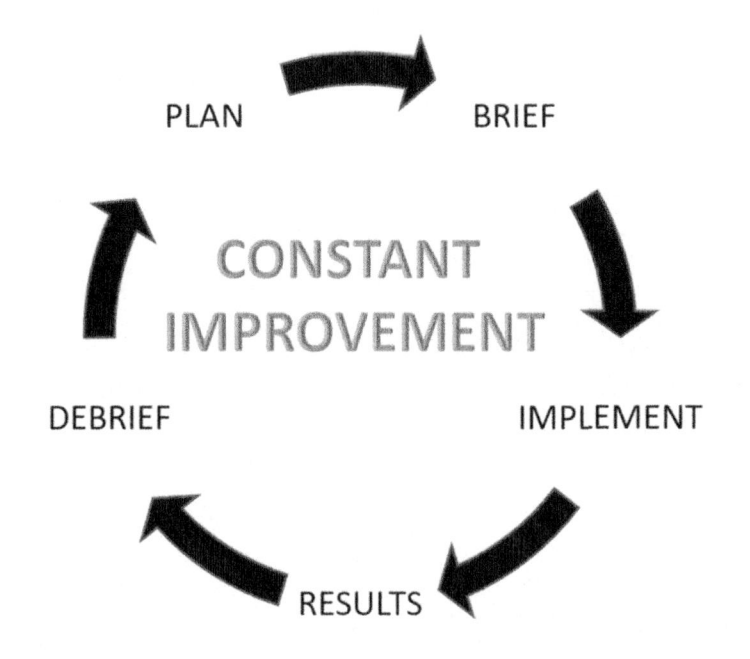

DEBRIEF — IMPLEMENT

RESULTS

Figure 16: The constant improvement cycle

Agile Marketing in a Turbulent Environment: How to adapt your marketing strategies to changing economic conditions.

"The essence of strategy is choosing what not to do."
- Michael Porter

The one thing that you cannot do as a business is just keeping on doing what you have always done. That will probably not deliver results for you.

You need to be able to pivot. Have the flexibility. Do not be afraid of trying new things – they may just pay off for you. Here's an example from the author's career.

We were approached by a new conference to take part. The author looked at their theme, their target audience, what was the potential value for us. A business case was written up and it was presented to the boss. He was sceptical, but the business case assured him that the £6,000 price tag should deliver at least one £150,000 opportunity.

We took the chance. We provided a break-out session as part of our deal. However, just before the event, one of the keynote speakers had to drop out for personal reasons. We were promoted to keynote, and at short notice found a different topic for our breakout.

At that conference we were the only company from our industry segment. We left that conference with opportunities in the seven figures – and we had a closure rate of around 35%. What a fantastic return on investment!

The following year the sales team were chomping at the bit. We rebooked, plus in a couple of other countries as the conference had launched in Paris, Frankfurt and Amsterdam too.

One of our competitors attended too as a breakout speaker. The ROI was not as high as that first year.

The third year, all of our sector competitors were there. They had seen our success and joined the party. The amount of noise we had to fight through was immense. There was also a commoditisation of our offering – not something that we wanted to be involved in.

The fourth year, sales complained and complained – the events were not on the calendar. The returns had sunk and strategically it was not the right thing to do. We needed to be leaders not in with the crowd. What did we do instead? We ran our own series of events with two complementary companies. Returns were high again. The first year we ran 6 roadshow events; the second year 40 across EMEA.

Then our competitors started their own roadshow events. The noise level was raised again. We wanted to stand out not be an also ran.

What did we do?

We went back to the conference series. BUT we did not go on our own. Instead we went with multiple complementary industry leading companies. We built the total data centre solution that the attendees were wanting. We stole the show.

We had moved away from the dangerous commoditisation problem, to being seen as an industry leading, well connected, proven solution provider. After all companies such as Cisco, EMC,

VMWare, NetApps and others wouldn't be attending an industry leading conference with a company that they didn't trust. Their reputation was on the line too.

If we had done what we always had done, then we would have been in the commoditisation battle. That would have impacted profitability, as products that are seen as commodities are bought and sold on price first and foremost.

Was it a risk? Yes, but a very calculated risk. During this time we moved from number 10 in the UK market to number 2. Just by daring to be different.

Think about the things that you have been doing year after year. Are they still serving you well? If yes, then great if they fit with your strategy. If the ROI is no longer there or your strategic direction has changed, then don't be scared of changing track.

The worst thing you can do is be stuck in your ways. At the same time, do not change things just because you think you should. Hopefully, the previous chapters have given you the tools to know what should be kept and what should go. Hopefully you have the confidence to stand up for what is right for your business, even if others want to keep the status quo.

Early in the author's career she had to break the news to a Regional Sales Manager that his six-monthly sales promotion was going to be cancelled. He was concerned that his sales would be negatively impacted.

However, the author had looked at the data. The sales promotion was aimed at the distributors. It was run like clockwork and guess what – the distributors waited for it to place stocking orders. This gave a peak twice a year, but for the 4-6 weeks ahead of the promotion, virtually nothing was purchased on the run-rate side, just major project orders. When sales guys went into the various branches they were out of stock of our products, and if they were requested, they were cross selling a competitors' that was in stock.

The Regional Sale Manager was still not convinced. He thought that the promotions were instilling loyalty. The author agreed to resign if in 6 months' time his sales were down (That is a card that has been played a couple of times in her career and have never resigned because of it yet).

The promotion didn't happen. The lull extended until the distributors realised that the sales promotion was not going to happen. Then they placed stocking orders. Not only that but they placed restocking orders. Sales actually went up overall, and the company saved the money of running the sales promotion.

It may seem a bit boring to look at the metrics and the data, but if they help you be profitable and hit your targets more easily, then you need to do it. Even if that means that you forget things that worked previously but are now not working as you want to work.

Don't always do things because you have always done them.

Don't do things because your competitors are doing them.

Instead take the time to see YOUR path through clearly and take your first steps in that direction. There is a lot of truth in the adage "Fortune favours the brave". Even in times of economic turbulence you can survive and thrive by knowing where your strengths are, identifying the opportunities and having the flexibility and agility to go for them.

Customer Feedback:

> *"Your most unhappy customers are your greatest source of learning."*
>
> *- Bill Gates*

As well as your staff giving you feedback in the debrief sessions learn how to listen to your customers.

Your customers, their needs, their success should be at the forefront of your mind.

These days with sites like Trustpilot, TripAdvisor or Google Reviews it is simpler than ever to get feedback. Do not worry if you have a criticism or a complaint, it shows others that you are being totally transparent with the reviews. But do ensure that the way that you dealt with the complaint, criticism or suggestion ensures that the customer remains loyal.

This example is from the author's experience to see how handling the complaint in a positive way was rewarded with not losing the client.

The author had purchased a dress from a concession in a department store, however, they had sold out of the optional belt to go with the dress. They directed to their store in the mall to see if they had it.

A visit to the store happened. There were two staff stood at the till chatting to each other. We stood and waited and then the husband interrupted them (he doesn't have a lot of patience for bad service, and we really didn't need to hear about one of their child's birthday party plans). Annoyed, one of the staff members pointed towards the back of the store.

We were the only people in the store. At the rear of the store there were two more staff standing chatting. There was only one belt out on display, and it was not the one for the dress.

Again we had to interrupt the gossiping, again it was as if we were an inconvenience and they cut us off when we were saying about the specific belt we were looking for and why. Apparently, they had all stock out. No offer to order the belt in.

We left, went next door and bought three belts and two dresses as the assistant listened. Not only did she show us what was on the shop floor, she also went to check what had arrived in that day's delivery.

Anyway, back to the poor experience. A tweet was sent to the first company saying how annoying the treatment by their staff was. Details of us being a silver tier loyalty card owner (i.e. a significant annual spend!).

A tweet by return asked for full details of the experience by direct message. Those details were provided, as if companies are not aware of failings, then they cannot be rectified. A direct message thanked for the feedback and asked for our address.

A few days later a letter thanking for my feedback and a £50 gift card arrived. Impressive! The complaint had not been filed to get money back.

What was really impressive though was the next visit to the store a few weeks later. There was a gentleman standing at the door, welcoming everyone. The author commented that that she'd not seen him before. His response was priceless:

> *"No madam I don't normally work at this branch, but we had had customer feedback that they staff here were not behaving to our company standard. They have been sent on training courses."*

Wow! He didn't know who had complained, how could he? It was a few weeks later and a busy Saturday afternoon. He was admitting that there had been a problem and it was being addressed to anyone who commented.

The company had taken my feedback and implemented the improvements needed. The result: A customer who felt very valued as a customer (and a little bit guilty for the trouble caused to those staff) and who remains loyal to the brand.

Work on turning your customer disappointments to loyal customers, just by the way you react to their feedback.

We have all come across people who ignore customer complaints (Just look at the Tesco example cited earlier in the book above). The author used to travel a lot as part of her job. There was one hotel owner who had mannerisms very similar to Basil Fawlty. He refused to acknowledge complaints – order poached egg on toast for breakfast – then the eggs turn up without toast. The toast follows 5-10 minutes later. Apparently, it was the customer's fault for not saying that they should be together. Poached egg ON toast was the order. This was in the days before TripAdvisor so he'd find it hard to behave like that now.

Strange how the bad experiences stay in minds for so long afterwards. You do not want that for your business.

Different ways of getting feedback from customers:
1. Ask for it on social media
2. Ask for a review on a third-party site
3. Conduct a "would you recommend us" quick survey, just as the NHS does with their "would you be happy for your loved one to receive care here?"
4. Suggestion box
5. The smiley face push button kiosks seen at various locations where you push one of five faces from very smiley to very angry looking – it is done as you walk by so an impulse response.
6. Conduct a Net Promoter Score Survey (more about that below)

Net Promoter Score is a way of monitoring how you are performing in terms of how likely your customers are to recommend you. The various survey software out there will have it as a question type. The question asks for a rating from 0 to 10, however, the NPS is not the mean average of the responses.

To calculate the NPS the scores are split as follows:

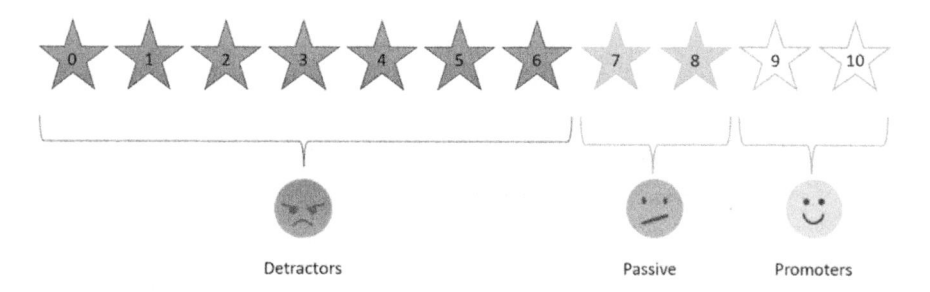

Figure 17: Net Promoter Score Categories

And the NPS is calculated by deducting the percentage of detractors from the percentage of promoters, those passive ones are ignored in the calculation:

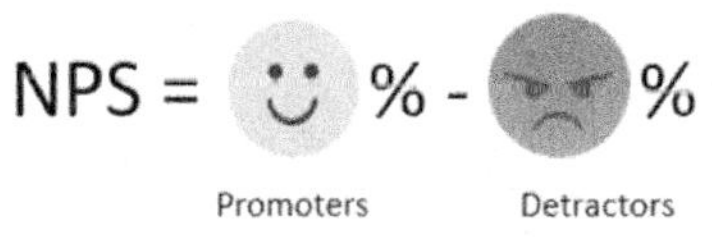

$$NPS = \text{Promoters}\% - \text{Detractors}\%$$

Figure 18: Net Promoter Score Calculation

So to put some example figures in there:

Rating	Number of responses	Category total	Category %
0	0		
1	0		
2	101		
3	22	378	25%
4	15		
5	165		
6	75		
7	450	839	
8	389		
9	267	295	19.5%
10	28		
Total Number	1512		
NPS Score	19.5%-25% = -5.5%		

Table 4: First Example of a NPS Score

Rating	Number of responses	Category total	Category %
0	0		
1	0		
2	101		
3	22	378	25%
4	15		
5	165		
6	75		
7	350	639	
8	289		
9	467	495	32.7%
10	28		
Total Number	1512		
NPS Score	32.7%-25% = 7.7		

Table 5: Second Example of a NPS Score

The difference between the two examples, is that some of the passives have been convinced to move up to 9 out of 10. Out of 1512 people just 200 moved giving a difference in the two scores of 13.2 and moving from a negative (where more people wouldn't recommend you) to a positive (where more people would recommend you).

If your score is between 0 and 20 then that is good, but there is still some room for improvement.

Above 20 is great and above 50 – wow you are excellent.

Look at the trend as well to ensure that you are improving.

Market Research

> *"To succeed, jump as quickly at opportunities as you do at conclusions."*
>
> *- Benjamin Franklin*

Market Research does not have to be complex to do. There are a couple of different areas of research, two different approaches, and two different levels.

Let's look at the approaches first: Qualitative and Quantitative. Yes, those two do have a lot of ts in them, but quite simple to differentiate between.

Quantitative is basically numbers, statistics, facts.

Qualitative is more opinions based.

On a written survey quantitative will be closed questions (yes / no / maybe, or a scale), qualitative will be open questions with text boxes for replies to be typed in. Or to get in depth qualitative you may run focus groups where the conversation is led by a facilitator to ensure that it is not dominated by one person, and the facilitator also asks the questions that should be discussed.

The two different levels are primary and secondary. Most market research will start with secondary research.

You do it every time you search on the internet.

You are looking at information and data that already exists and you may use a wide variety of sources but are also mindful of which sources you can trust and which maybe not so much.

Primary research is something that you devise and run yourself. It may be a questionnaire, it may be a series of focus groups. It is a lot more time consuming to do, but it can be very valuable and give you credibility (remember the section about market intelligence above spoke about surveys. It does mean that you get the answers to the specific questions that you have which you may not be able to have answered by secondary research.

Now let's turn to the areas of research. The most common ones include competitor analysis, product need, and background information (PESTLE analysis).

Competitor analysis

I've lost count of the number of companies who tell me that they don't have a competitor, and it may be true that they don't have a 100% match of a competitor, but there will still be companies who compete albeit indirectly.

If you sell kitchens, then your competitors could be companies such as Wren, Holdens, Magnet, B&Q and Wickes or handmade bespoke kitchens. They seem obvious enough, don't they? But with the sale of a big-ticket item such as a kitchen there are other things that the £10,000 - £150,000 could be spent on – a car, paying down the mortgage, building an extension, new windows, solar panels, a once in a lifetime holiday.

You need to look at both direct competitors and indirect. Those who are targeting the same audience as you for the same monetary spend.

Take a look at their offerings, their messaging, what their ideal customer looks like, which vertical markets they concentrate on, their reviews, website, strengths, weaknesses, what their turnover was at

Companies House (if a limited company), number of staff / branches, lead times, warranties offered ...

You are NOT wanting to copy them, but if you spot an opportunity in a different vertical market or you can close a gap with your offerings that they don't have, then it gives you opportunities without competing on price.

Very early in the author's career she worked in the refractories industry (heat and wear resistant bricks and things). We would compete with some companies on some materials, but also supply them with other items they didn't produce. You may need to be careful with that due to laws around cartels and competition / antitrust, but if you compete fairly where you compete then there is nothing wrong with also being a supplier of different products or services to a company.

Think about a software company who is developing a CRM product. That same company may be using Microsoft 365 and PowerApps, even though Microsoft also sell Microsoft Dynamics CRM.

PESTLE

This is really six areas in one, and each letter stands for a type of knowledge that a company needs to have.

Political: what is happening politically can severely impact business. Think back to autumn 2022, three prime ministers in a matter of weeks. The mini-budget chaos. It's impact on interest rates and overall business confidence. Now in 2024 there is an election looming and the impact that has on the markets.

But election years can be more specific to you if you sell heavily into the public sector. When there is an election announced much spending is moved into purdah – i.e. between the announcement and the formation of a new government in the UK much public spending stops. Normally, that is a few weeks – 6 weeks for the election and then on election night the victorious PM is in place and things move on. However, think back to the 2010 election. There was no clear winner, and it took 5 additional days before a Government was in place. Northern Ireland and the Assembly not sitting for months at a time – various devolved service areas basically stop.

Economic: unemployment levels, salary levels, interest rates, raw material inflation, overall inflation. All of these and more have an impact on a business. As depressing as it can be listening to the news during economically turbulent times, it is something that you do have to have an eye on.

Socio-cultural: what are the trends out there and how should you respond, if at all? How are the politics and economic conditions influencing social and cultural activities? If you are a gym owner, it could be that with the cost-of-living crisis that memberships are being cancelled. It may be that since Covid people want more open-air activities, so how can you facilitate that? As a newsagent the decline in the number of smokers over the last few decades has reduced a revenue stream for you – how do you fill that gap?

Technological: are there new tools out there that will help speed up your processes, whether 3D printing for prototypes or ChatGPT for social media post writing? Knowing what is going on in your sector, plus around cybersecurity, is key so that you don't get left behind or subjected to a fatal ransomware attack.

Legal: Laws change, as any property landlord or bank will tell you. There are also laws around Net Zero, how you can use environmental claims in your marketing (they have to be provable). But it could be something like the National Living Wage or the retirement age (when the author started work a woman retired at 60, then it was raised to 65, then 67). Being aware of employment law is also key for anyone with employees. There are also Health & Safety laws that are updated. Not being aware of a law change or introduction is not a defence.

Environmental: This is a big one and will be getting ever larger as the effects of climate change become ever more apparent. Moving to Net Zero. Replacing plastic from packaging to something more sustainable. Moving to electric fleet vehicles from diesel, or if you have a fleet of HGVs moving to biodiesel or hydrogen, ships are moving to hydrogen. Every business will be impacted. Customers are looking for the green option – recycled polyester, fewer food miles, stating that responses to a tender can only be made by ISO14001 holders or BCorps.

Product Need & Market Sizing

Just once in her consultancy has the author had to turn to a client and say that his product would not payback the investment he had already spent developing it. It was a painful conversation, and really the research should have been done first to save him over £40,000 of his pension savings.

Look at what is already out in the market. Ask people what they would want from your product – what would need to be in an MVP (minimally viable product), what they would really like to see and what would be nice to haves.

Research the price points that your ideal customer would be willing to pay.

Look at where the market is today in terms of size – Statista[28] has a lot of good quality freely available market sizing data, they have more behind a paywall, but you don't necessarily have to go there.

The EU also have a lot of data available, you may need to dig around a bit.[29] There are then industry specific reports out there covering a wide range of products and services.

What you want to find out is how big is the market, what percentage of the market do you want to go after, what will that take to do and what will that provide in terms of revenue?

Like lots of areas of marketing, do not do research for the sakes of doing research, but do the research that is going to help you make the correct business decisions. You do not want to end up with analysis paralysis.

---

[28] https://www.statista.com/

[29] https://data.europa.eu/data/datasets?locale=en

Conclusion

> *"People don't buy what you do, they buy why you do it."*
>
> – Simon Sinek.

Over the course of the preceding chapters hopefully you have been inspired that there is a lot that can be done with marketing to help your business not only survive but also thrive without investing a lot of, if any, money.

More importantly, by looking at all angles of the marketing mix then, you will have a well-rounded company with a strong strategy in place to really rocket when the good times return.

Whether that is defining and putting processes into place allowing expansion and quicker onboarding of new starters, or really knowing what your ideal customer looks like and where they get their information so that you can tailor where messages are sent out. Reducing the amount of work done but targeting it with laser focus for better results.

The author sincerely hopes that you use this book time and again to help you get to where you are going. That you now see the value of having a good marketing in place, and that it is not all promotion and advertising.

Wishing you and your business much success.

Index

6 Ws, 52
   How, 56
   What, 52
   When, 53
   Where, 52
   Who, 52
   Why, 54

Abandoned carts, 174

Ad blockers, 96

Advertising, 43, 50, 119, 121
   Bus, *121*
   Display Online, *119*
   Offline, *120*
   OOH (Outdoor), *120*
   Radio, *123*
   Taxi, *120*
   Tube, *122*

Agile Marketing, 179

Airbnb, 24

Aldi, 26

Amazon, *132*, 164

Amazon Prime, *107*

American Express, *151*

American Marketing Association, 43

Analysis Tools, Social Media, *81*

Apple, 36

apprentices, 29

Are there any quick fixes?, 25

Argos, *151*

Articles. *See* PR

Avast, 96

Back links, *101*

Backlinks, *132*

BANTS, *110*

BBC, *101*

BCG. *See* Boston Consulting Group

BCorp, 51, 62

BCorps, 195

Bing, *95*

Black Friday, *153*

Blog, *100*, *104*

Bloggers, 87

Blogs, *127*

Boosting, *91*

Boston Consulting Group, 34
Bounce rate, 174
Bow-tie relationship structure, *147*
Boxpark, *133*
Breakout, *140*
Budget Holder, *63*
budgets, 33
Buffer, *83*
Buyer, 61
buyer persona definition matrix, 58
By-line. *See* PR
Case Studies, *128*
  SCRAP, *130*
cash cow, 34
cashflow, 33
Chambers of Commerce, 30
channel partners, 29
ChatGPT, *105*
CIPS, *143*
Cisco, *163*, 180
Citrix, *137*
click through rate. *See* CTR
closed questions, 191

commoditisation, 180
Communication Flows, 77
Competition. *See* Insurance Backed Competition
Competitor analysis, 192
competitors, 35
complaint, 183
Conferences, *139*
confidence, 16
Conversion rates, 175
Corporate Social Responsibility, CSR, *103*
cost per acquisition. *See* CPA
Cost per click, *95*, 173
cost per conversion. *See* CPC (Conversion)
cost per thousand. *See* CPM
Costs of referrals, 175
CPA, 172
CPC, *95*
CPC (Click), 173
CPC (conversion), 173
CPM, 173

Creator Mode, *83*

criticism, 183

Croydon, *133*

CTR, 173

Customer Experience, *149*

Customer Feedback, 183

Customer Service, *149*

CyberMonday, *153*

DA. *See* Domain Authority

data, 182

debrief, 176

Decision-Maker, *65*

Deep link, *101*

Defining your target audience, 57

demographics, 57

DFS, *153*

Diamond Relationship Structure, *147*

Direct mail, *115*

Distributors. *See* Place

DMU, 61

Domain authority, *101*

Domain Authority, *132*

Dwell time, 173

E books, *132*

eBay, *151*

Economic, 194

economy, 15, 16, 18, 19, 20, 24, 26, 35, 121, 143

elevator pitch, 36

Elizabeth Line, *122*

Elon Musk, *87*

Email Marketing, *109*

EMC, 180

encourage ideas from everyone, 41

Engagement, *80*

Environmental, 195

environmental change, 42

e-privacy, *109*

ESG, 40, 51, *62*

ESG, Environmental Social Governance, *103*

Esso, *151*

EU, 196

Events, *133*

Evri, *80*

Excel, The, *133*

Exhibitions, *134*

Exhibitor – in person, *135*
Exhibitor – online, *134*
Walk through, *134*
Extranet, *107*
EY, *143*
Facebook, 87, *91*
Facebook Live, *80*
Farmfoods, *117*
Flexibility, 40
focus, 35
focus groups, 191
Followers, *80*
forecasts, 33
Foundation, 31
Freevee, *107*
Friends Reunited, *88*
FTSE100, *137*
Gated Content, *106*
Gatekeeper, *64*
GDPR, *84*, *109*
GK Barry, 57
Google, *100*
Google Ads, *95*
Google Reviews, 183
GoogleForms, *144*
Gucci, 37

hard measurement, 169
Hashtag, *81*
Hashtags, *84*
Hashtag Volumes, *86*
higher wages, 19
Hootsuite, *83*
horizontal markets, 60
HubSpot, *112*, *113*
ICO, *109*
ideal customer, 57
IMC. *See* Integrated Marketing Campaigns, IMC
IMF, 20
inflation, 16, 19, 20, 25, 26
Inflation, 17
Influencers, *149*
Initiator, *64*
Instagram, 87, *91*
Insurance Backed Competition, *153*
Integrated Marketing Campaigns, IMC, *161*
interest rates, 16, 20, 26

Internal Marketing, *157*

Intranet, *107*

ISO14001, *62*, 195

Journalists, *87*

Keynotes, *139*

Keywords, *95*, *99*

KFC, 57

Landing page, *104*

Lead nurturing, *110*

leads, 172

Legal, 194

lifetime value. *See* LTV

LinkedIn, *82*, *91*
  Company Page, *83*
  LinkedIn Lives, *84*, *140*
  LinkedIn Newsletters, *84*

Listen, 42

Local Government, 29

London Liverpool Street, *133*

Long tail searches, *99*

Looking at your other customers, 27

loyalty card, 184

Loyalty Schemes, *151*

LTV, 172

M&S, *152*

Mailchimp, *112*

MailChimp, *113*

MailerLite, *114*

Maltese Cross, *116*

Malware, *96*

Manchester Piccadilly, *133*

margins, 33

Market Intelligence, *143*

Market Research, 191

Market Sizing, 195

Marketing in Turbulent Times, *75*

Marketing Measurement and Adaptation, 167

marketing mindset, 44

Marketing Mindset, 43

marketing Ps, 44

Marketing Ps
  People, 45, 49
  Physical Evidence, 45, 49
  Place, 44, 47
  Planet, 45
  Price, 44, 46
  Process, 45, 50

203

Product, 44, 45

Promotion, 44, 49

Mastodon, *87*

McDonald's, *153*

metrics, 182

minimally viable product. *See* MVP

Mission & Vision Statements, 35

mission statement, 39

Mission Statement, *103*

Monopoly, *154*

Moz, *101*

MS365, *142*

MS-Forms, *144*

MS-Teams, *142*

MVP, 195

Myrie, Clive, *80*

MySpace, *88*

Nectar, *151*

Negative growth, 20

Net Promoter Score, 186

Net Promoter Score Calculation, 187

Net Zero, 45, 194

NetApps, 181

Netflix, 37

Network Rail, *134*

New followers on LinkedIn, *83*

Newsletters, *112*

NHS, 186

NPS. *See* Net Promoter Score

numbers, 33

Off page SEO, *101*

offerings, 33

On page SEO, *101*

OOH (Outdoor). *See* Advertising

open questions, 191

Opinion Pieces. *See* PR

opportunities, 172

Oxfam, 40

pandemic, 15

Panduit, *163*

peer-to-peer lending, 23

Persona Development, 61

PESTLE, 193

Pinterest, *88*

pipeline, 172

Podcasts, *132*

point of sale. *See* POS

Political, 193

political uncertainty, 17

Pop-up Stand, *133*

POS, 164

PowerPoint, *138*

PR, *100*, *125*, *143*
   Articles, *127*
   By-line, *127*
   Opinion Pieces, *127*
   Press Releases, *125*

Press Releases. *See* PR

price, 25

Primary research, 192

Product Need, 195

profitability, 33

Qualitative, 191

Quantitative, 191

questionnaire, 192

QuestionPro, *144*

real costs of someone being in the office, 41

recession, 13, 16, 17, 18, 19, 21, 24, 27, 158

Reels, *81*

Referral Fee, *149*

referrals, 28

Referrals, *149*

Relationship marketing, *112*

Relationship Marketing, *145*

Resellers. *See* Place

Responsive website, *101*

Retailers, 29

return on advertising spend. *See* ROAS

return on investment. *See* ROI

Rhythm, 40

ROAS, 173

ROI, 172

Royal Mail, *116*

S&P, *143*

Sainsbury's, 26, 42

Sainsburys, *151*

sales promotion, 181

Sales Promotions, *153*

sanctions, 17, 19

save, 42

SCRAP. *See* Case Studies

Search engine optimisation, *99*

secondary research, 191

sectors, 18

segments, 57

SEM, *95*

Semicon West, *135*

Seminars, *135*

SEMRush, *99*

SEO, *99, 132*

Shoreditch, *133*

Sinclair C5, 44

Sky, *107*

SMART Goal Definitions, *71*
   Attainable, *72*
   Measurable, *72*
   Relevant, *73*
   Specific, *71*
   Timely, *73*

SMART Marketing Goals, *71*

SmoothFM, *123*

SnapChat, *88*

social media, 25

Social Media, Organic, *79*
   Customer Services, 80

Social Media, Paid For, *91*

Socio-cultural, 194

Soft measurement, 169

Source, 174

Sparks, *152*

Spiders, *100*

stakeholders, 27

Statista, 196

Strategic Alliance, *163*

Streamyard, *84*

strengths, 182

suggestion, 183

suppliers, 28

supply chain, 15

SurveyMonkey, *144*

Surveys, *143*

Sustainability, 45

Swan Vesta, 41

targets, 35

Technical Advisor, 61

Technological, 194

Tesco, 26

Tesla, *154*

Testimonials, *131*

TfL, *134*

Theodore Levitt, 43

Threads, *87*

206

TikTok, *81*, *88*
Tonka Toy, *137*
Top exit pages, 174
Top pages, 174
tribes, 57
Tri-fold, *116*
TripAdvisor, 183, 185
Trustpilot, 183
tweet, 184
Twitter, *87*, *91*
Uber, 24
Ubersuggest, *99*
Ukraine, 16, 17, 19
Unilever, 40
Unique Selling Proposition, 67
Unique Selling Proposition (USP), 56
Use the winds to your advantage, 22
User Experience, *104*
Users, 62
utility bills, 19

V shape, 15
Value of sales, 172
Value Proposition, *67*
vertical markets, 60
vision statement, 39
Vision Statement, *103*
VMWare, 181
war, 19
Warby Parker, 39
Webinar, *84*, *100*
Webinars, *140*
Website, *103*
What is Marketing, 43
What's In It For Me?, 68
Whistl, *116*
White papers, *100*
White Papers, *131*
WIIFM, 68
Word of Mouth, *149*
Workshops, *135*
X, *87*, *91*
Zoho Campaign, *112*

Printed in Great Britain
by Amazon